HOOKED

HOOKED

write fiction that grabs readers at
page one and never lets them go

Les Edgerton

WRITER'S DIGEST BOOKS

writersdigest.com
Cincinnati, Ohio

Visit our Web sites at www.writersdigest.com and www.wdeditors.com for information on more resources for writers.

To receive a free weekly e-mail newsletter delivering tips and updates about writing and about Writer's Digest products, register directly at our Web site at http://newsletters.fwpublications.com.

11   5

Distributed in Canada by Fraser Direct, 100 Armstrong Avenue

Georgetown, Ontario, Canada L7G 5S4, Tel: (905) 877-4411; Distributed in the U.K. and Europe by David & Charles, Brunel House, Newton Abbot, Devon, TQ12 4PU, England, Tel: (+44) 1626 323200, Fax: (+44) 1626 323319, E-mail: postmaster@davidandcharles.co.uk; Distributed in Australia by Capricorn Link, P.O. Box 704, Windsor, NSW 2756 Australia, Tel: (02) 4577-3555

Library of Congress Cataloging-in-Publication Data
Edgerton, Leslie.
  Hooked : write fiction that grabs readers at page one and never lets them go / Les Edgerton. -- 1st ed.
      p. cm.
  Includes index.
  ISBN-13: 978-1-58297-457-6 (pbk. : alk. paper)
  ISBN-10: 1-58297-457-8 (pbk. : alk. paper)
  ISBN-13: 978-1-58297-514-6 (hardcover : alk. paper)
  ISBN-10: 1-58297-514-0 (hardcover : alk. paper)
  I. Fiction--Authorship. I. Title.
  PN3355.E34 2007
  813'.54--dc22   2006101971

Edited by Kelly Nickell
Designed by Claudean Wheeler
Production coordinated by Mark Griffin

F•W PUBLICATIONS, INC.

DEDICATION

This book is dedicated to all the writers who didn't give up, no matter how long the odds or how fierce the struggle or how much the naysayers scoffed at their labor. To those who through their sweat, blood, and toil become our conscience and our heart and our soul, and who continually elevate us all as humans. You are a special breed, and I love you all.

ABOUT THE AUTHOR

Les Edgerton lives with his wife, Mary, and son, Mike, in Fort Wayne, Indiana, where he writes full-time. He has been the writer-in-residence at the University of Toledo for the past three years.

He has two daughters: newlywed Britney, who works in the computer industry in Louisville, and Sienna, who is a housewife and mom in Edwardsburg, Michigan.

Les writes short stories, articles, essays, novels, and screenplays. His fiction has been nominated for the Pushcart Prize, O. Henry Award, Edgar Allan Poe Award (short story category), Jesse Jones Award, PEN/Faulkner Award, and the Violet Crown Book Award. One of his screenplays was a semifinalist for the Nicholl Fellowships in Screenwriting program, a finalist in the Austin Film Festival Heart of Film Screenplay Competition, and a finalist in the Writers Guild "Best American Screenplays" Competition. One of his short stories appeared in Houghton Mifflin's *Best American Mystery Stories of 2001.* This is his eighth book, and he is currently hard at work writing two new books, another one on writing and one on baseball.

Those interested can keep up to date with his new work at his Web site at www.lesedgerton.com.

ACKNOWLEDGMENTS

I've been fortunate to have had a number of books published, and, in each case, have enjoyed the services of a good editor. But my editor on this particular book—Kelly Nickell—has been an editor of rare and uncommon talent. Without a doubt, Kelly has been the toughest editor I've ever had the good fortune to work with, as well as the very best. They keep telling us there are no more Maxwell Perkinses these days, but I'm here to testify that his spiritual descendent is very much with us in her personage. She is just one crackerjack editor and whatever value this book contains, she is responsible for a great deal of it, much, much more so than if I'd been left to my own devices.

I really got lucky with this one! Besides Kelly, this book also enjoyed the expert touches of one of the best copy editors around, Nicole Klungle.

Thanks also to the editor who saw the value of this book and signed it up, Jane Friedman. Jane, I hope you feel your faith was justified!

And, to all the folks at Writer's Digest who worked "behind the scenes" on the work that bears my name—I appreciate your efforts and I hope you think of this as "your" book also ... for it is.

TABLE OF
CONTENTS

CHAPTER THREE

CHAPTER FOUR

CHAPTER FIVE

CHAPTER SIX

CHAPTER SEVEN

CHAPTER EIGHT

CHAPTER NINE

CHAPTER TEN

CHAPTER ELEVEN

EPILOGUE

INDEX

FOREWORD

The All-Important Beginning

If you were to accuse Les Edgerton of being an expert on the subject of fiction writing he would most likely blush with embarrassment and tell you in his delightful Southern manner that he's merely sharing his own experiences and passion for the writing life, but thanks anyway, ma'am, for the compliment. He's the only writing teacher I've ever encountered who can matter-of-factly start a sentence with "When I was a hair stylist," "When I was in prison," and "When I taught at three universities simultaneously."

This richly textured—and unexpected—background allows Les to write with the same colloquialisms that pepper his speech. In his previous book, *Finding Your Voice: How to Put Personality in Your Writing*, he encourages writers to break "da rules" taught by "Missus Grundy at P.S. 101" and find their own unique voice. This book is a supremely informative text that's often laugh-out-loud funny. College professor meets vaudeville comedian.

I met Les Edgerton serendipitously (or not) while preparing for my own course, called The Voice of Essence, at the Esalen Institute in Big Sur, California. After I cruised the Web, scanning dozens of titles, his book popped out as exactly what I needed to augment my curriculum. I devoured *Finding Your Voice* without leaving my chair and promptly tracked down his e-mail address to dash off a note of praise. Within minutes I received a lengthy, friendly note in return, saying that he read my e-mail out loud to his wife, Mary, just to show her he has fans "out there in California." Before long he was coaching me on my new novel and I was critiquing screenplays and stories written by him and several of his students. He has become my secret weapon—the writing guru I always enjoy quoting—when leading workshops of my own.

In his second guide for writers, *Hooked: Write Fiction That Grabs Readers at Page One and Never Lets Them Go*, he grabs us from page one, giving us important information and insight in a format that's entertaining and accessible. He refers to the inciting incident as "the trouble thing" and tells us "It's daggoned hard to write scenes." He asks us, "With me so far?" and advises us to stick our fingers down our throats and ralph up those clichés. And yet, beneath the humor is a scholarly work designed to guide writers through those difficult opening chapters. Les knows that crafting a novel is hard work, and he'll be the first to say so. His respect for those brave enough to attempt the novel is on every page. He believes anyone with the fortitude to complete a novel can actually do it, yet he steers clear of empty promises. In *Hooked*, you will be treated to a comprehensive education about the all-important beginning of a novel or a short story and have a really good time along the away. A textbook that's also a page-turner. What a novel idea! I can't wait to recommend this book to every writer I'm working with, just as I enthusiastically encouraged them to keep *Finding Your Voice* in their permanent libraries.

—LISA LIEBERMAN DOCTOR

Lisa Lieberman Doctor enjoyed a sixteen-year career as a motion picture development executive at such companies as Universal Pictures, Warner Brothers, and TriStar Pictures. Her last executive position was Vice President of Robin Williams' company, Blue Wolf Productions, where she oversaw production of *Mrs. Doubtfire*. In 1995 she switched gears to become a staff writer on ABC's *General Hospital* and its spin-off, *Port Charles*. She was nominated for a Daytime Emmy and Writers Guild Award for her work as part of the *General Hospital* team.

INTRODUCTION

Why a Book on Beginnings

Why a book on just story *beginnings*? The simple truth is, if your beginning doesn't do the job it needs to, the rest of the story most likely won't be read by the agent or editor or publisher you submit it to. A better question is why only *one* book on beginnings! It is very possibly the most important part of the story you'll write, and you need to get it right if you want your story to see print.

A tremendous number of manuscripts never get read by agents and editors. Wait. Amend that to: A tremendous number of *possibly good and even brilliant novels and short stories* never get read *beyond the first few paragraphs or pages* by agents and editors. Why? Simple: The stories don't begin in the right place. When an agent or editor encounters a poor or improper beginning, she doesn't bother to read on. This book intends to help writers fix that problem.

That's the entire premise of this book. Sounds simple, doesn't it? It *is* simple, and yet, other than being written in the wrong voice (check out my earlier

I

Writer's Digest book, *Finding Your Voice*, for valuable information on voice), the single biggest reason manuscripts get rejected is because the writer begins in the wrong place. What's ironic is that manuscripts don't get rejected because the majority of the story is good and only the beginning is flawed—they get rejected because the agent or editor *never gets to the good part to begin with*. A story that begins in the wrong place won't be read much past that point. If the good stuff occurs later on, in all likelihood it will never be reached by the agent or editor.

So, how does it happen that writers bury the good stuff, and agents and editors never get to it? I'll tell you.

Writers bury the good stuff because many, if not most, writers are never taught how to begin stories or even how to structure stories at all. Many writing classes focus on writing *exercises*. Parts of writing. Chicken nuggets instead of the full roasted bird. A unit on how to write descriptions, for instance. Another on how to create character. Or, one on effective dialogue. And so on. But very little is actually taught as to how stories are put together. And even less is passed on about the most important element of story structure—the beginning of a story.

In the few instances when story structure is taught at all, more often than not the model offered is an archaic one. It's the one the teacher herself learned years ago when she was a student, and she is just passing it on to the next generation.

What the teacher doesn't realize is that writing evolves, and what's accepted today is different than what was acceptable even a few short years ago. Much different.

This book is going to show you what's acceptable these days. What agents, editors, and (ultimately) readers expect.

Once you know what's acceptable, your work is going to get read. All the way through.

If you bury the good stuff, failing to start your story with the good stuff, an agent or editor won't keep reading your manuscript. They are usually drowning in manuscript submissions. There's not enough time for them to read all the work they receive, plus perform the hundreds of other duties the job requires. In defense against that mountain of manuscripts, they figure out ways to *not* read manuscripts. At least not entire manuscripts. How? They develop a list of red flags that signal to them that the novel or short story submission they've just opened isn't going to be worth their limited reading time. Each editor will have her own such list, but just about all of them share one universal red flag. Almost to a person, they will put down a manuscript that starts out in the wrong place. Experience teaches them that reading a story begun wrong is almost always going to turn out to be a serious waste of time. So, they simply don't.

How do I know this? For one thing, because I've been an editor for a couple of anthologies, a guest editor of the annual *Flying Island*, and an associate editor for a wonderful literary magazine, the *Crescent Review*. As an editor, I learned more in a month about what it takes to get published than I did in any writing classes in school.

Once I sat behind that editor's desk, barely able to see over the Mount Everest of manuscripts awaiting my perusal and my decision to recommend them for publication or to reject them, I quickly got a clear idea of why good beginnings are so crucial. It took less than a day behind the editor's desk for me to figure out that boring beginnings or beginnings that were obviously wrong were going to lead to poorly written stories a very high percentage of the time. The way submitted material begins is almost always indicative of what's to follow.

The first thing I realized was that there was no way on earth I was ever going to get through that pile of manuscripts heaped up before me if I read every page of every blessed one of 'em. Not unless I wanted to give up other activities in my life. Activities like eating, sleeping, brushing my teeth, going to the bathroom, saying hello to my significant other, acknowledging those cute little munchkins roaming around the house. ... Even if I gave up those things, I was still not going to find enough time to reduce that paper mountain to at least a foothill.

So. What did I do?

Simple. I did what just about every other editor and agent has found herself doing. I created a list of little red flags that told me when it was time to put a manuscript down and go on to the next one. (I'll address how to correct five major red flags in chapter nine.) There are the obvious flags that everyone goes by, such as improper format, misspellings, punctuation mistakes, grammar and syntax mistakes, inconsistent point of view, a manuscript that has obviously been to several places because of its physical condition, etc. And then, of course, there's the bad beginning. The truth is, if I came upon a story that had a great beginning—and they're relatively rare—I knew from just a little bit of experience that the odds of discovering a good, quality story had just increased exponentially. I was even more amenable to ignoring other red flags, or at least to tolerating them better, and to reading on. See, that's the thing about good beginnings: They prompt the editor to read at least a bit further. *Great* beginnings buy the writer a lot of leeway further on in the story, believe me.

Doesn't it make sense to gain those bonus points with an editor?

The good news is that great beginnings aren't difficult to master.

What is really neat about all this is that starting stories off where they should begin and in a way that makes agents and editors and readers sit up and take notice isn't a difficult thing to master at all. What's even cooler about all this is that once you learn what constitutes the proper beginning to your stories, you're going to be leagues ahead of your competition, and your manuscripts are going to start getting published. You'll end up with a little thing called a writing career. Awesome! And it couldn't happen to a more deserving person, could it!

One quick sidenote. I will never refer to a story in this book as a piece. As in: "When you begin to work on your piece ..." I suspect that's a significant part of our problem as writers in getting our work published. Our terminology sometimes reflects our mind-set about our work. We're so used to receiving writing instruction in precisely that way—in pieces—that we even refer to the thing we're working on as such. Writing education, by and large, consists of far too many exercises, in my experience. The teacher gives us a unit on description, then one on something called characterization, then one on ... You get the picture. We learn *pieces*. This approach, in and of itself, isn't necessarily a terrible thing, but what is perhaps terrible is that many times the teacher neglects to show her students the big picture. The story itself. How it's shaped. It's not just throwing a bunch of pieces together. It's much more complicated than that.

I have my own theory about why writing is taught largely through exercises: It's easy.

It's easy to tell the class, "Okay now, boys and girls, today we're going to work on descriptions. For the rest of the hour, I want you to come up with an original description of a beach. You know, like crashing waves, burnished sand dunes, wind with a salt tang in it. *Original* stuff like that." (I'm being sarcastic with that last sentence, in case you missed it.) Then, with the class happily engaged—well, *busy*, anyway—the teacher can do her important work, which is to sit back and read a novel and keep an industrious eye on the clock.

You may feel that, since this book is purported to be about only story beginnings, I am violating my own precept. Trust me, I'm not. A good, quality story beginning is a microcosm of the work entire. If you capture the right beginning, you've written a small version of the whole.

BEGINNINGS DEFINED

Now, before we get into the specifics, let's explore the different types of openings just to make sure we're all on the same page: There's the opening line, the opening paragraph, the opening scene, the opening page, and the opening chapter itself. All of these, except the entire first chapter, are included in a proper opening. Many times, these different types of openings do constitute the entire first chapter, but not always. Just as many times, the opening is only a part of the first chapter, like when the author departs from the opening scene and goes into a sequel and/or a flashback, which is usually signaled by a space break (we'll discuss transitional techniques in chapter ten). Or when the opening is completed and a new, important character is introduced, also normally signaled by a space break

Here, in our time together, we'll focus on the story opening itself, which is advisedly the most important part of most stories and the area perhaps most neglected and misunderstood. After all, if you don't begin properly, is it practical to assume those first readers who decide publication status will read further? As you'll see, improper openings pretty much doom manuscripts to being put down fairly quickly. Not a fate you want for your hard work!

Be aware that the "rules" for story openings have changed from even a few years ago. We'll get into the reasons for that in chapter one. Suffice to say, for now, that many of the great books from the past aren't practical structure models for today's market, particularly in the way some of those books begin. As Bob Dylan reported, "The times, they are a-changin'."

Not to worry—within these pages lie the principles for writing great beginnings. Beginnings that compel the gatekeepers of publishing to keep reading!

Let's get to work.

CHAPTER ONE

Story Structure and the Scene

Now, the *practical* stuff! Let's look at how successful stories are structured these days and how they got that way.

In one important way, stories have remained unchanged since Aristotle first reported on 'em. And he was talking about a structure that had been around for eons before he wrote it down on parchment. There are—now, as well as then—three basic parts of a story. They are—you guessed it!—a beginning, a middle, and an end. "Once upon a time" goes on until "they lived happily (or, *unhappily*, depending on your bent) ever after."

What's not done today is the immediate helping of backstory right after that (implied) "once upon a time." We don't fill readers in on the protagonist's life for the past ten years leading up to the story's actually beginning. We also don't spend a lot of time describing the village he lives in, the street he walks down each day to work, his waking habits, or the copious details of each room he enters. Or every bite of the breakfast he ingests or the primary colors of the songbird outside his window.

No sir. No ma'am. Not anymore.

THE EVOLUTION
OF STORY STRUCTURE

What is considered proper story structure has many times changed, and often changed drastically. For instance, Samuel Richardson's *Pamela* (also known as *Virtue Rewarded*) is considered by many to be the very first published novel (printed in 1740), and that alone qualifies it as a classic; but alas, novels written in the epistolary style *Pamela* was written in are considered fairly archaic today and pretty much unpublishable. While that is an extreme case, it does illustrate why many of the revered books in history may serve as poor models for stories written today.

Novels and short stories, no matter how complex their plots may appear, are almost always based on a simple underlying structure: A character begins in stability in his world; this world becomes unstable after the introduction of an inciting incident; the character struggles to restore his stability; and a new stability is established at the conclusion, reflecting the change the protagonist has undergone as a result of the struggle. Almost a mathematical formula: Stability + Inciting Incident = Instability + Struggle to Resolve Instability = New Stability. Very succinctly, a story is a movement from stability to instability to a new stability.

What is different about today's story structure is that the first part of the equation—stability—has been shortened considerably and, in many cases, completely omitted. In literary eras past, the present of the character, or even the past (the backstory), could be leisurely developed before the second part of the formula, the inciting incident, occurred. Today, that period of stability is far shorter and may consist of only a sentence or two—and sometimes not even that. Many times that period of former stability is only implied, or is discussed only later on in the story.

Christopher Moore's novel *Island of the Sequined Love Nun* (which is studied much more thoroughly in chapter five) is an excellent model for the new structure of novels—it begins smack in the middle of the inciting incident. No preamble, no backstory, not a word of description of the stability that existed before the inciting incident.

I have called beginning with the inciting incident a new structure, but there are ancient examples of this structure as well. Consider Sophocles' play *Oedipus Rex.* The stability of Oedipus is that he is king of Thebes and married to Jocasta. In the *very first scene*, the citizens of Thebes approach Oedipus and tell him a terrible curse is on the land—bad things are happening everywhere. This is his inciting incident. He now has a story problem: He has to end the plague on his kingdom—the widespread starvation caused by the crops failing, etc. During the struggle that ensues, he comes to learn that he himself is the cause of the curse, and that knowledge causes him to change profoundly and emerge with a new stability, both for him and his kingdom. The starvation of his people ends and they gain a new stability, and Oedipus finds his new stability as a wandering beggar.

Take note that Sophocles doesn't waste time in establishing Oedipus's character at the beginning, other than to note that he's the king. He throws him directly and immediately into the fire.

Another of the ancients—Homer—begins his epic poem *The Iliad* with the inciting incident, and not with backstory or the stability that exists before the inciting incident. *The Iliad* begins with the line: "Rage—goddess, sing the wrath of Peleus' son Achilles." This is the inciting incident—the beginning of Achilles' story problem. He's angry because Agamemnon has taken a slave woman Achilles believes rightfully belongs to him. His world (stability) is changed (made unstable) by Agamemnon's act. Can't get a better inciting incident than that!

These are a couple of the ancients who understood how to open a story properly. They would each probably fare well today against the competition of television and movies and iPods.

Somehow, in the years since they first wrote, authors went backward a few stumbling steps, and decided that readers weren't as smart as they were in Homer's and

Sophocles' day, and that they needed to bring their customers up to speed by delivering lots of backstory/setup or the readers wouldn't "get it."

Thankfully, we seem to be realizing that our readers are pretty smart cookies and don't really need all that crapola.

Some of the so-called masters who wrote since those days created the kind of novel Mark Twain may have been thinking of when he said, "A classic is something that everybody wants to have read and nobody wants to read."

THE MODERN STORY STRUCTURE

As noted above, we now begin a story when the trouble that's going to be the focus of the story first occurs. All else is prologue, and we call that stuff backstory and setup. Get that in later, once the story problem is established. Here's the basic contemporary story structure:

1. **Inciting incident.** A scene in which something happens to the protagonist that creates his surface problem and introduces the first indications of the story-worthy problem. This is where today's stories begin. Covered extensively throughout this book!

2. **Struggle to resolve the surface and story-worthy problems.** The balance of the rest of the story involves the protagonist's struggle to resolve the surface and story-worthy problems despite the obstacles the antagonist throws his way to prevent him from reaching that goal.

Note that the initial surface problem can lead to other surface problems, but each new surface problem must arise organically out of the preceding problem.

3. The resolution of the story. This is usually defined as the point when the character either achieves or fails to achieve his goal. I think we need to redefine that. That definition leads writers to believe that they need to deliver endings that either allow the protagonist to win the prize or to lose it. Not an accurate description of a good ending at all. Actually, all good story endings and resolutions should involve both an element of a win and an element of a loss. Tidy endings that represent a clear-cut victory or loss just aren't very good endings.

Let's look at the movie *Thelma & Louise* for a great example of an ending that contains both a win and a loss. The struggle that both Thelma and Louise face is against male domination. At the end, the two women decide to drive their Thunderbird over the edge of the Grand Canyon to certain death. The loss? Pretty obvious—death. The win? They've achieved their freedom from men. They've chosen to live their lives (at least for the few brief seconds remaining after their decision) on their own terms, free at last. One powerful ending indeed!

As you can clearly see, good endings aren't always defined as simply "goal achieved" or "goal not achieved," but more accurately as "satisfactory," meaning they contain a balance of win and loss.

This is the structure of the contemporary short story and novel. What we're going to deal with in these pages are what good openings are and how to create them.

SCENE BASICS 101

Now that we've taken a brief look at the evolution of story structure, let's break it down a bit further and examine the scene. Everything of importance in a story should be rendered via a scene. A scene is simply a unit of dramatic action. That means people doing things—speaking, interacting, performing actions. And it means conflict. Always conflict.

Before we get to opening-scene specifics, let's take a look at the dynamics of a standard scene. This type of basic scene requires several things. It needs at least two characters who are at odds with one another, even if their conflict is muted or under the surface or revealed in subtext. Preferably these two characters are the protagonist and the antagonist. The protagonist is the character we follow in the story. The antagonist is the person whose goals conflict with the protagonist's and who therefore provides the opposition to the protagonist's efforts to resolve his story problem. The antagonist can be just as "good" a character as the protagonist. In fact, the higher the quality of the antagonist's goals, the more complex the story becomes.

These two characters and their conflicting goals provide the tension that's central to every story. A protagonist should not gain anything easily. This is one of the toughest lessons for a writer to learn. In real life, you probably do everything in your power to avoid trouble or to reduce it whenever possible. In fiction, however, you need to seek out trouble for your protagonist at every possible opportunity. Even if he only wants a street address, make it hard to get! Each scene in a story is a battle, and the story entire is a war.

Once the story is underway, the structure of most scenes is as follows:

1. The protagonist enters the scene with a goal. That goal is to begin some action designed to resolve the story problem. The scene itself can take many forms. It may be a scene in which the protagonist attempts to gain information to help him resolve the problem. It may be a direct action intended to resolve the problem.

2. The antagonist also enters the scene with a goal. The antagonist's goal will be in conflict with the protagonist's.

3. The scene ends in disaster for the protagonist. Leave your protagonist in worse shape than when he entered the scene and further away from resolving the story problem. Basically, get your protagonist in a miserable place and then make it worse. Get the character up a tree (in trouble) and throw rocks (obstacles) at him. Don't let him off the hook even for a second. He can get close and even gain a part of the answer, but he can never fully resolve the problem by the end of a scene—until the final scene. The first time a scene ends in success—resolution of the goal—the story is over. The protagonist can achieve a partial victory—in fact, most scenes do end with a partial victory. But only the final scene of the story can end in total success.

4. **The story continues after the scene ends.** Once the scene ends, you can then go into backstory, exposition, summary, character rumination; all that stuff most of us are dying to do. That's called sequel, and it follows scene. For a great discussion of scenes and sequels and how they work together to make up the building blocks of fiction, check out Jack M. Bickham's *Scene and Structure* from Writer's Digest Books. I consider this book my bible and quite possibly the best practical book on writing structure ever written.

OPENING SCENES VS. NON-OPENING SCENES

Now that you understand the structure of a basic scene, let's take a look at opening scenes and how they differ from their non-opening counterparts.

A typical non-opening scene begins with the protagonist, or at least the scene's focus character, entering with a specific goal. Something he wants to accomplish. That can take the form of virtually anything, but whatever the goal is, it must be tied directly to the protagonist's effort to resolve the story problem.

Because of its specific goals (outlined in chapter two), the opening scene has a unique structure not found elsewhere in the story. Think of it this way: The opening scene is the dramatization of the inciting incident—what happens to the protagonist that creates the initial surface problem and sets the stage for the story-worthy problem to develop. This is the only scene in the story that the protagonist doesn't enter with the goal of resolving some type of problem, and that's simply because it's the opening scene's job to create the initial problem in the first place. In other words, before this scene, there's no problem to resolve, therefore the protagonist can't enter it with a goal.

The motivation to do something to help resolve the problem is the main area of difference between the opening scene and those that follow in the narrative. Most opening scenes don't contain any motive; rather, they focus on the motive's inception. Thus, the opening scene is virtually the only time the protagonist gets to be reactionary. After this opening scene—after the inciting incident—the protagonist has to very quickly become proactive to resolve the problems.

Note, too, that the opening scene is itself a significant exception to the rule that scenes require at least two characters. Why? Because many opening scenes center around dramatic events that happen to the protagonist while he is alone or when he is the only character present who is truly involved in the story. We'll look at a great example of such a scene in chapter six, when we discuss James Baldwin's short story "Sonny's Blues." (There's no rule saying that your antagonist cannot be present in the opening scene, but if your antagonist is present, don't begin the opening scene from his point of view. After all, this scene is about your protagonist and the inciting incident.)

There the differences between opening and non-opening scenes end. Like non-opening scenes, opening scenes are usually followed by a sequel, in which you can get inside your protagonist's head to show the readers his reaction to what's just happened. When the opening scene ends (in disaster), the sequel begins with the character's emotional reaction, going from that emotion to the intellectual portion of the mind, where a new action is formulated. A new scene begins as soon as the character begins to implement that action.

The Dangers of Opening
With Summary Instead of Scene

Opening with a character mucking about in his own mind, ruminating and contemplating his navel, pon dering the meaning of life or the intolerable political system he happens to be suffering under or the abuse he suffered at the hands of his next of kin, is the kiss of death. Guaranteed. No matter how skillful the author, "telling" via exposition just can't do the job of opening a story nearly as powerfully as "showing" through a dramatic scene can.

The problem with a character rambling about in his head to deliver backstory is that it's all summary. It's all *telling* the reader. My students do this all the time, until they find out it's unacceptable. They groan and they protest at first, but after their complaints fall on deaf ears (mine), they give out a long sigh and buckle down to the hard work of writing actual scenes. For many, it's the first time they've been required to do so. They've floated by in high school and even college classes by writing stories that are mainly summary.

Summary doesn't convince anyone of anything. *Write that down*. It's as true as anything ever was true.

Your goal is to evoke an emotional response that hooks the reader, and telling absolutely won't get it. The reader must live through that opening scene right along with the protagonist. This is the only way the reader will really believe it and, more importantly, *feel* it.

No story should ever begin with a sentence like: "The day Francine walked in and discovered the dead body of her husband Frank was the day her whole life changed." That's *telling* the reader something has affected Francine.

And what happened to Francine won't matter in the least to the reader, who will mostly likely put down the story shortly after reading this sentence. Writing such a sentence is an example of not trusting the reader to "get it" (we'll talk more about this subject in chapter two). An occasional reader might read a bit further, but I can almost guarantee you that an editor or an agent very likely won't bother to read the second sentence. You can't tell him a character is in trouble—you have to *show* him.

If you're guilty of beginning stories with reveries about your character's bad luck or crummy childhood, or about how his significant other was and is a dodohead, look over those paragraphs you wrote. I'll bet a large amount of money that's when you trotted out all the adverbs and adjectives and clichés, and all the flowery, elevated, pseudopoetical, abstract language you were capable of. All the ten-dollar words you knew or could look up in a dictionary or thesaurus. That should begin to tell you something.

You're trying to punch up the emotion with language. *You* probably see the scene in your head, but you're not writing the scene you see—only the narrator's *description* of that scene and the emotions *you* feel from it. You've lived through the scene in your imagination, but you probably forgot the reader hasn't. With me so far? You need to share that scene with the reader, because that's the only way the reader is going to experience the same emotion you do. If your writing resembles what I just described, stick your finger down your throat and ... do it. *Ralph*. Preferably all over those insidious pages. Just get it out of your system. It's poisoning you as a writer. Now you're ready to continue.

PROLOGUES

Prologues are often just a section of backstory or setup relabeled as prologue. It ain't foolin' nobody, chum. Sorry. It's just the same wine in a slightly different bottle. If it looks like backstory or setup, walks like backstory or setup, quacks like backstory or setup—then it's Donald-the-Backstory/Setup-Duck. Setting it apart and calling it something else isn't going to work. Here's some advice on prologues:

Mostly: Don't do 'em.

There are, of course, exceptions. One popular exception is a prologue in a book in an established series. A prologue is sometimes used in such a book simply to bring the fans of the series up to speed for the current read. Many times, it will include a short synopsis of where the protagonist was when the previous book ended—and perhaps a major shift he has undergone offstage since the previous story.

There are other legitimate reasons to employ a prologue. But don't use one if you're just trying to sneak in backstory. If that's the sole reason for writing a prologue, it's probably best to forego the prologue altogether.

A Word About Epilogues

Nor would I recommend writing epilogues in most cases. They are usually a bad attempt to fix a poorly written ending. Kind of like the vaudevillian trick of accompanying a bad joke with a rim shot.

Are epilogues sometimes acceptable? Well, sure. Sometimes. It's a case-by-case scenario. If the only reason you write one is to tie up a bunch of loose ends, to answer a dozen story questions not addressed by the "real" ending, then you might look to rewrite your story so those questions are answered earlier by a better story ending. In most novels, subplots and other minor story questions and problems are resolved before, or, even with, the main problem the plot is built around.

However, too many times, epilogues are an effort to help out the reader—to make sure the reader "gets it."

Don't do 'em—not for that reason!

CHAPTER TWO

Opening Scenes: An Overview

The opening of a short story or novel is just that—the very beginning. That's the simple and straightforward definition. However, what this book is really concerned with is illustrating the differences between good and bad openings—although perhaps it may be best not to assign words like *good* and *bad* to openings. Instead we're going to be talking about and describing openings that work and openings that don't work.

THE COMPONENTS OF AN OPENING SCENE

An opening scene has ten core components: (1) the inciting incident; (2) the story-worthy problem; (3) the initial surface problem; (4) the setup; (5) backstory; (6) a stellar opening sentence; (7) language; (8) character; (9) setting; and (10) foreshadowing. Let's take a quick look at each and how they work together to help the opening scene achieve its unique goals. This is only an overview, as these elements are discussed in greater detail in later chapters.

The Primary Components

Each of the ten components is important, but some are more important than others. The four most important, in almost all stories, are the inciting incident, the story-worthy problem that is introduced by the inciting incident, the initial surface problem that is directly created as a result of the inciting incident, and the setup. The importance of the last six ingredients varies according to the individual story, but even though important, they usually take a back seat to the first four.

1. The Inciting Incident

As noted in the previous chapter, the inciting incident is the event that creates the character's initial surface problem and introduces the first inklings of the story-worthy problem. In essence, this is the "action" part of the story, the part that is plot-based. This happens to the protagonist, then he does this to resolve it, then this, and so on.

2. The Story-Worthy Problem

The inciting incident sets the stage for the story-worthy problem, which functions just beneath the surface of the story on a more psychological level. Consider it

Chapter Two

the driving force behind the initial surface problem as it's ultimately what the protagonist must reconcile at the end of the story. The inciting incident introduces this problem by either bringing to the forefront a buried problem or creating a new one, thus beginning the gradual revealing process that will encompass the rest of the story as the protagonist's—and the reader's—understanding of the true nature of story-worthy problem deepens.

3. The Initial Surface Problem

This is the problem that occurs as a direct result of the inciting incident. And while it may seem at first glance that solving this problem is what the story is really all about, it's not. As we just discussed in the previous section, every story is ultimately about solving the deeper, more complicated story-worthy problem that is slowly revealed as the story progresses. So why does the initial surface problem qualify as a primary opening scene component? Simple. It propels the protagonist to take action (he wants to solve it, or at least he better for your story to work), and assists in the eventual revelation of the story-worthy problem.

Keep in mind that the initial surface problem can evolve into or create additional, even larger surface problems, but that these must rise organically from the initial problem and always be firmly moored to the story-worthy problem.

4. The Setup

The definition of the setup is just that—it "sets up" the opening scene by giving a snapshot that allows what will take place in the following scene to be clear to the reader. The last thing you want to happen is to force the reader to "backtrack" to make sense of what's taking place in the scene. That's why opening directly with dialogue is usually a mistake. Unless the dialogue is crystal clear as to who's talking to whom and about what, the reader may have to go back and reread the dialogue again once she figures out the context and who the participants are and their relationship to each other. At the least, such backtracking—either literally or on a subconscious level—represents a speed bump. At the worst, it can create a complete stall for the fictive dream. There are, of course, exceptions, but it's usually safest to not take chances and to avoid beginning with direct dialogue.

Setup can take any number of forms or combinations of forms. The overall "rule" is to only give what's absolutely necessary for the reader to understand the scene that will follow and no more. Remember, this is the beginning and the beginning is the place the reader will decide whether to invest any more time in the story. That means little or no backstory—save that for later. (That's why I've listed backstory as a secondary component instead of primary component despite that fact at least a small amount usually appears in opening scenes—to remind you to use it with care.) You also shouldn't include excessive detail or description in your setup. Save it. Your setup *should* contain at least a hint of the trouble to come, either directly or indirectly. It may be something as simple as showing the reader a man and a woman seated across from each other in a restaurant and the man refusing to meet the woman's eyes as she begins talking. At the other extreme, it may need to show that the restaurant is an abandoned, dust-covered dining room in a Western ghost town and it has recently been designated as an atomic bomb test site. In any case, only provide the bare minimum that will serve the scene that follows and orient the reader sufficiently that what ensues is clear as it begins to take place.

The Secondary Components

Now that we've defined the inciting incident, the story-worthy problem, the initial surface problem, and the setup, all of which make up the foundation of an opening scene, let's look at the secondary components of backstory, a stellar opening sentence, language, character, setting, and foreshadowing. I say secondary because, while the first four ingredients are absolutely crucial to any beginning, these last six take on varying degrees of importance depending on the story and your aims, and some of these latter components may not even appear in some openings.

5. Backstory

This is usually where new writers err the most when it comes to their opening scenes. Backstory includes anything and everything that's happened up to the time of the inciting incident. There are times when a bit of backstory is necessary for the reader to grasp what's going on in the inciting incident and why it's important. However, this is the greatest bane for most editors and agents when they encounter a newly submitted manuscript and is the biggest kiss of death for the work. Tread carefully when considering how much backstory to include in your story.

Are there times when a longer backstory is necessary? Actually, there are. In many police procedurals, mysteries, thrillers and related genres, the story begins often with a crime being committed. The protagonist is nowhere around the scene at the book's beginning. Many of best-selling novelist John Sandford's novels are classic examples. They begin with the crime being committed and it's only later that the protagonist enters the story.

There are other exceptions, such as in Larry Watson's *Montana 1948*, which we'll look at in chapter four.

The danger in telling you that backstory can sometimes be lengthy, is that you may take that as license to provide too much backstory. The single biggest fault of most writers is that they simply don't trust the reader's intelligence to "get" what's going on without providing lengthy backstory. Editors, agents, and writing teachers constantly fight that impulse in writers. Many writers feel the reader has to know that Mary has been married three times, each relationship ending badly, to "understand" why she's looking for a good relationship. Providing that kind of backstory will most likely lead to rejection and is the kind of backstory that, while indeed important, needs to be doled out at a later point in the story and bit by bit.

In general, keep backstory either absent from the opening or only include as much as is absolutely necessary to set the scene for the inciting incident. We'll discuss backstory in greater detail in chapter four.

6. The Opening Line

Spend an awful lot of time on this sentence. In fact, more effort should be expended on your story's first sentence than on any other line in your entire story. No kidding. The first sentence is the first thing the readers will see when they open the door of your manuscript or story. Make sure it's a good 'un! One that will create a strong impression. My own favorite is one I used in my short story "The Bad Part of Town," which begins: *He was so mean that wherever he was standing became the bad part of town.*

I know it's my own story and one should at least appear to be somewhat humble, but honestly, do you think most readers would be able to resist reading on after reading that sentence?

7. Language

The opening is where you should create your most memorable language. The first sentence is often the best sentence of all in many successful stories. Take time to craft not only the first sentence, but the rest of the opening. Refrain from using adverbs and too many adjectives, especially ordinary ones. For gosh sakes, don't pair adjectives in an attempt to make the description more powerful. The rule of thumb with adjectives is that with each additional one, the power is halved, not doubled, as many mistakenly think. The secret to good writing is to employ strong, original verbs (avoid forms of *to be*), and concrete nouns. Avoid "invisible" words like *beautiful* or redundant phrasing like *ran quickly*. Especially avoid using adverbial qualifiers for dialogue tags; instead, stick to *said* for almost all of your tags.

8. Character Introduction

The opening is where you at least introduce your protagonist and usually the antagonist. This doesn't mean you give a life history for either of these principle characters. Introduce your reader to your characters by showing the characters' reactions to the inciting incident. Those reactions reveal and define their personalities, creating a first impression as strong as any in our own lives.

Brevity is key here. Instead of long, boring physical descriptions and little tangential stories that you think will illuminate your character's personality, pick a telling detail and let the reader fill in the rest. Characters are best revealed by their actions instead of exposition anyway, and you have a whole, entire book or story for exposition. For instance, if you feel it important to develop your protagonist's characterization as a skinflint, don't give some long, drawn-out tale of him pinching pennies as a youngster, or (worse!) tell the reader he's a miserable miser. Instead, in your opening scene, show him *doing* something miserly within the context of the inciting incident scene. Show him having to transfer two handfuls of hundred-dollar bills to one hand so he can scoop the inside of the coin return of a candy machine for forgotten nickels. Remember, you don't have to develop the whole of his characterization in the opening—just the single most important facet—and you should do that briefly and with a telling action.

Also be careful not to introduce too many characters at once. Give your reader time to get to know the main character(s) before flooding the page with many others. A host of people parading about on the stage when the story has scarcely begun will confuse the reader, who will be trying to keep track of all these folks. If there are very many characters in the beginning, your reader may well throw up her hands at trying to figure out who all these people are and how they may impact the story.

9. Setting
At least a glimpse of the setting should be included in the opening. It's important to be grounded physically. The

amount of detail you provide should depend on how important the setting will prove to be. Writers like Ellen Gilchrist and Raymond Chandler made their story settings almost a character in their stories, and so included greater detail than did the minimalist Raymond Carver, who was much more interested in character. The setting includes many things—the physical space from the doily on the end table to the Milky Way and beyond. The time period is part of the setting. The culture and society the characters find themselves in is also a part. Anything that can be seen, heard, or imagined is an element of the setting. Be careful that you only include details that are important. To paraphrase Chekhov, if a gun appears on the credenza in act one, it needs to be fired by act three. All that means is that every detail in the setting has to serve a purpose. The reader will expect whatever is being described or noted about the setting to play a prominent part somewhere in the tale.

Keep in mind that setting is one of the ingredients that may or may not be that important, and it is hardly ever as important as many writers believe it to be. Sometimes writers spend far too much space on creating the setting because, well, settings are easy to write. Half the time you've spent in English and writing classes has probably been devoted to writing settings. You become good at them. The problem is, when you have a strength, it's tempting to go to it again and again, instead of tackling the tough part of writing, which is writing scenes. Also, description has changed a lot from the days you learned how to write description in school. Today, passive description is largely eschewed, and almost all description in a contemporary story is active description, incorporated unobtrusively within the action of a scene, so the bit of description doesn't stop the scene or even slow it down noticeably.

In yesteryear, you may have been praised by your teachers for long paragraphs of near-poetic descriptions, using clever similes and metaphors and laying on the language of dead poets. But today's description is short and sweet, and doesn't interfere with the action and drama of the scene. Instead of describing a highway's "thin, white hypnotic lines" or "bumper-to-bumper traffic with little kids and dogs hanging out of windows" and the like, today we would simply write something like Tim Dorsey did in his hysterically funny novel *Torpedo Juice*: "His headlights bounced off a panther crossing sign."

However, there are times and stories that do call for more extensive settings—specifically, stories in which the setting becomes a character itself. Many of Ellen Gilchrist's stories depend on the city of New Orleans playing a character's role. Faulkner's fictional Yoknapatawpha County setting is as much a character in several of his novels as any flesh-and-blood person. That duly noted, Faulkner still didn't open his stories with detailed descriptions of place, but rather waited until a bit later to deliver lengthy descriptions.

For most stories and novels, a brief description of setting is useful and even necessary to ground the reader, but I urge you to save lengthy descriptions for later on. A brief description of setting is important, and it is important that it be brief.

10. Foreshadowing

Foreshadowing is hinting at the action or obstacles to come. Hints about upcoming perils create page-turning reads, but foreshadowing may or may not be important in your opening. For certain types of novels—mysteries and thrillers, for instance—foreshadowing may be very important. For other genres it may not even be necessary. Let's say you have a character who will save the day at the end by leaping over a tremendous chasm. You may want to foreshadow that in the very beginning by mentioning that he won the bronze medal in the long jump in the 1984 Olympics. Even though that initial mention may occur on page 1, and he doesn't actually make the big hop until page 387, the reader will remember and the jump won't seem ludicrous when he actually makes it. It will have been effectively foreshadowed.

These are the major components or elements a good opening scene should include, and we'll be discussing them again and again throughout the book. Only you can determine which of the ten components need to be included in your story, and to what length. Think of the top four components as first tier, and the last six as second tier.

These ten components are a lot to have going on in a relatively short space, so it's key that you write tight. The opening scene should be relatively short—a good working length would be one to four pages—so it's important to be concise and make the language work in more than one way. (We'll take a closer look at length in chapter ten.)

THE GOALS OF OPENINGS

The opening of your story carries an awesome responsibility, and the ten core components outlined in the previous pages work together to make sure your opening meets reader demands. The goals of your opening scene are: (1) to successfully introduce the story-worthy problem; (2) to hook the readers; (3) to establish the rules of the story; and (4) to forecast the ending of the story. If your opening fails to accomplish any one of these elements, then guess what—your opening will be faulty at best and unreadable at worst. To ensure, then, that your opening doesn't have any lethal lapses, let's take a closer look at each of the opening obligations.

1. Introduce the Story-Worthy Problem

This is the opening's most important goal of all. In fact, its importance cannot be overstated. Without a proper story-worthy problem, your story doesn't have much chance of success. I'll go into greater detail on this later on, but for now the story problem is, well, it's the heart and soul of the story. After all, a story has no reason whatsoever to exist unless it's about trouble, and the story-worthy problem is that trouble. The majority of the novel or story, then, contains the protagonist's struggle to resolve this problem. You must set the stage for the story-worthy problem's eventual unveiling (remember, it's revealed gradually throughout the story rather than all at once like a surface problem) right from the get-go to give the reader a compelling reason to keep turning the pages, and this is done via an inciting incident, which is the event that triggers the protagonist's initial surface problem and sets up the story-worthy problem.

It's important to pause here and note that the word *trouble* in fiction terms doesn't carry the same definition as it does in real life. A wife leaving a husband, someone losing a job, a murder next door or even in the protagonist's own household don't, by themselves, qualify as trouble in fiction terms. *Trouble*, in literary terms, means the protagonist's world has been altered profoundly by some event—not altered in terms of material or surface things, such as a loss of income, the death of a loved one, or an injury—but in terms of the inner psychological world of the character being significantly changed for the worse. For instance, the loss of one's job and perhaps even livelihood, while fairly drastic in real life, isn't enough to sustain a story. However, if the character has tied his sense of self to his profession, then losing a job can easily represent an inner psychological problem and be transformed from merely a bad situation into a story-worthy problem.

Just as a story about characters who experience only good things in their lives is boring to everyone except, possibly, close family members and friends, a story about people to whom bad things happen but with no effect on their inner psychological selves is just as boring. It's like driving by a horrible car accident—you may feel a twinge of pity for the victims, but not enough of a twinge to pull over, defy the police officers trying to establish order, and walk up and find out everything you can about what happened. (At least not very many of us would.) The same thing is true in fiction. A character with a Job-like existence isn't really all that interesting, but when we find out his sorry existence is caused by a deity testing his faith and his battle to maintain it or even fight its loss, then the story suddenly becomes interesting.

2. Hook the Reader

Perhaps not every single successful story has a hook, but it's fairly difficult to name one that doesn't. A hook is something that intrigues the reader, and it can be virtually anything that makes the reader want to read further. It can be a story question—will the protagonist overcome the daunting problem confronting him?—or it can be the lovely language of the author, or any of a dozen and one other things. In short, anything that can draw the reader in can serve as a hook.

What most good hooks have in common is that they have strong inciting incidents that plunge the protagonist immediately into trouble—the trouble that's going to occupy the rest of the story. There are a few rare authors who can compel the reader to invest her time with solely the beauty of their prose (think John Updike), but you shouldn't rely on your facile command of language to draw in the reader. The surest way to involve the reader is to begin with an opening scene that changes the protagonist's world profoundly and creates a story-worthy problem. Even Updike, as great a stylist as he is, doesn't rely only on his ability to create memorable prose to hook his readers; he begins with trouble.

A good hook can have other facets to it. Here's one hook that operates on several levels, from Jo-Anne Michiel Watts' short story "What's Not to Enjoy?"

> A few days before Thanksgiving I get a terrific recipe from the Turkey Hotline Lady while Dyna and I make love.

What a superb opening! Who could possibly resist reading on? There are questions galore in this opening. First, what sort of person not only remembers getting a "terrific recipe" while making love, but places more importance on the recipe than the sexual act itself? What kind of person even notices recipes she overhears on the radio while making love? Why is it important for the author to mention specifically that this happened just before Thanksgiving? Also, we know from the byline that this is a female writer, and so the narrator may be a woman. Yet the first-person account has her talking about a lover named Dyna, and this may well be a female name. Are the lovers lesbians? While it may be politically correct to pretend to not notice such things, or, if we do notice them, to not comment on them, we're all still human and have a curiosity about such love affairs, no matter what our sexual orientation is, straight or gay. (As it turns out, Dyna is a male, but we don't know that at this point in the story. There's at least a question about the narrator's sexuality.) Or, perhaps Watts is taking the persona of a man in this story—yet another reason to read on to find out if that's what she's doing.

And then, the language itself draws us in. There's intelligent, understated humor in this first sentence, and that tells us that this story will likely make us at least smile, always a good feeling to have when encountering a story. "The Turkey Hotline Lady" is just plain funny—one of those terms that make adults smile, just as the word "poop" makes little kids (especially little boys) smile. Further, Watts employs a conversational, colloquial style of language that gives us the sense that a friend is relating the tale to us.

Watts' opening is a great example of a hook that does just what hooks are meant to do: draw the reader in and make him want to read more. Where's the trouble in Watts' opening, you may ask. Well, the fact that the narrator/protagonist chooses to report on a recipe rather than on lovemaking tells us there's trouble in River City, to borrow a phrase from *The Music Man*.

3. Establish the Story Rules

Each novel or short story has certain rules—rules you, as the author, must establish and convey to readers so that your story can be read intelligently. These rules can be almost anything you desire, so long as they follow one ironclad dictum: They must be consistent. That means, for instance, that you can't begin your novel by writing somberly about serious stuff, and then switch on page 30 to a black-comedy treatment of the material. You have to establish what kind of story it's going to be from the very beginning. In other words, don't try to fool the reader. She won't forgive you for that. However you begin the story—voice, tone, the way the story is narrated—that's the way it has to continue up to and through the ending. Consistency is key to the writing of a good novel. When readers jump on the train, they expect and hope for surprises, but not in this area.

That brings me to another important point: The beginning must be connected to the whole of the story. That may seem to be common sense and not worth mentioning, but remember that you should never write an opening that is only marginally related to the story itself solely to create a hook to draw the reader in. For instance, if you were to begin a story with scores of alien spaceships attacking Earth, and your intrepid hero rushing to NASA headquarters to tell them he's discovered that water makes the aliens melt—and then you have him wake up and it was only a dream, you would be guilty of tricking or manipulating the reader, who has come to expect something entirely different from the promise of that beginning, even if the dream is somehow tied to the initial surface problem. No reader will forgive you, and no reader should.

4. Forecast the Ending

The ending? "I thought this was a book about *openings*," you say. It is, but the beginnings of the best stories very often contain at least a hint of the ending. As T.S. Eliot said, "In my beginning is my end." When students approach me, stuck on how to end their stories, my first advice is to look back at their beginning, for the answer should lie there. A good example is my own short story "It's Different," which begins:

> As a boy, he had watched his mother grow bigger with the child that would become his sister. The larger her belly grew, the more repulsed he became, shrinking from her touch, afraid to touch her skin. Two reasons:

She might explode, expel the thing inside her. Her skin, the skin on her upper arms that had gotten thicker, felt cool, clammy. Skin that enveloped fatness.

Now, he had one himself. A pregnant wife.

The character finds he can't relate to his wife's pregnancy, the proof of that culminating when she attempts sex with him and he's unable to respond. When she goes to sleep and he gets up and begins doing the crossword puzzle in the paper, a combination of words comes up that leads him to the realization that his relationship with his mother has led to his revulsion toward his wife during her pregnancy. It comes full circle when he remembers his own childhood and the feelings he had and what caused those feelings. The seeds of your ending can often be sown in your beginning. Begin with just a brief hint of what's to take place at the end, and you'll create a story that feels complete to the reader.

WHY POTENTIALLY GOOD BEGINNINGS GO BAD

Perhaps the primary reason we begin our stories in the wrong place is that a great many of us haven't learned yet to trust the reader's intelligence. This is the real key to understanding just about all of the problems that lead to the wrong beginnings, not to mention many of the other problems with creating sound, quality stories. Stories that, among other things, involve the reader in a true reading experience—a participatory exercise that's much more enjoyable than a story in which everything is laid out for the reader and the reader isn't required to bring anything to the table (i.e., one brain, armed with a decent IQ). Once you understand the concept of trusting the reader's intelligence, then poor beginnings, as well as many other problems that prevent stories from getting published, will begin to disappear.

Of course, it is important to note here that the opening scene is the only one developed within a vacuum. By that, I mean that later scenes benefit from the knowledge conveyed in previous scenes, knowledge that helps orient the reader in the scene and helps the reader understand what's going on with the characters. Not so the first scene. Unless the novel is part of an already-established series, the reader knows nothing about the situation or the characters. Thus, the writer's temptation to furnish a lot of backstory and setup to bring the reader up-to-date is valid, but nonetheless incorrect. Readers don't need to know everything about your characters in order to understand what's going on when the stuff hits the fan (during the inciting incident), and they don't need to understand what led to the situation in order to fully realize the significance of what's happened when the trouble begins.

Intelligent readers understand a lot from a tiny bit of information. Give them credit for having functional brains. For instance, let's say you want to write a story about a man who has something happen to him that reveals to him that he needs a healthy relationship with a woman to be complete, but he's been married and divorced five times in his life, strong evidence that he sucks at relationships. His backstory is that he's been married five times. The setup is that he's now alone after his last failed marriage. A writer with little trust in her reader's intelligence may feel that she needs to take the reader through those five marriages to show how miserable her protagonist is at relationships. Or perhaps this writer decides she doesn't have to describe all five marriages, but describes only one, maybe the last one.

This is a story that won't get read. The skillful writer won't describe the failed marriages. She'll simply include the fact that the man's been married five times. The intelligent reader will infer from this that the protagonist is a guy who fails at relationships.

CHAPTER THREE

The Inciting Incident, the Initial Surface Problem, and the Story-Worthy Problem

First, it's imperative that you understand what stories *always* have to be about. One thing and one thing only.

Trouble.

That's it. Period. There is simply no reason for a story to ever exist unless it's about trouble. There are very few absolutes in fiction, but that's one of 'em. As we've discussed in the previous chapters, the inciting incident creates trouble in the form of the initial surface problem, which then helps to manifest the protagonist's story-worthy problem—the problem that's going to be revealed throughout the duration of the story.

If stories are always about one thing and one thing only—*trouble*—then the story shouldn't really begin at any time other than when the trouble begins. The story simply doesn't exist before that point. Anything before that is backstory or setup (we'll discuss both of these in great detail in chapter four).

Trouble in the literary sense comes in two forms: story-worthy problems and surface problems. It's important to note here that one type can't exist without the other. They must be solidly linked in order for your story to work. If you discover that there is a disconnect, then your surface problem needs to be adjusted until it's organically and directly linked to the story-worthy problem.

The story-worthy problem is always the paramount problem; it's what the story is really about in the final analysis. As you'll see later in this chapter, a true story-worthy problem is closely associated with the protagonist's inner self, while a surface problem is merely symptomatic, derivative of that larger problem. Also, since a surface problem may change and mutate and lead to new problems throughout the course of your story, your protagonist might struggle to resolve multiple surface problems, although the story-worthy problem will remain consistent throughout (we'll look at this topic later, as well).

In this chapter, we're going to examine the inciting incident and both the initial surface problem and the story-worthy problem, as well as the protagonist's goals for each.

THE INCITING INCIDENT

The inciting incident must be written as a scene. A *dramatic* scene, not a *melodramatic* scene. For readers to understand and grasp the protagonist's emotion, they have to live through it right along with him. It won't work at all to tell readers what's happened via summary, exposition, or the character's memories of the event delivered via internal monologue (thoughts). Always remember that everything important in a story needs to be written as a scene. Stories must affect readers emotionally first and foremost, and the only way you can effectively create emotion in readers is through a scene. The moment the protagonist becomes aware of the initial surface problem and is forced to take action is one of the most important aspects of a story, so it goes without saying that it needs to be delivered as a scene.

A scene is a unit of drama. Drama means conflict. And this is where many writers go wrong. They often confuse conflict with melodrama. I see this in my younger writing students all the time. When you say "conflict" to them, their television- and movie-influenced sensibilities go to things like gunfire, murder, fiery car crashes, bloody fistfights, kidnappings, graphic rapes, strident and volatile arguments, and the like. They're thinking of *physical* conflict. Usually, that translates into melodrama and not true drama. Drama reaches down inside to the very heart, soul, and psyche of the individual. Melodrama is almost always about the external and superficial. Melodrama is shrieking vs. the quiet and deep truth of drama.

As Janet Burroway says in her wonderful text *Writing Fiction: A Guide to Narrative Craft*:

> ... the protagonist must want, and want intensely. The thing that the character wants need not be violent or spectacular; it is the intensity of the wanting that introduces an element of danger.

About melodrama vs. drama, Burroway goes on to say:

> Another mistake frequently made by young writers is to think that they can best introduce drama into their stories by way or murderers, chase scenes, crashes, and vampires, the external stock dangers of pulp and TV. In fact, all of us know that the most profound impediments to our desire usually lie closer to home, in our own bodies, personalities, friends, lovers, and families. Fewer people have cause to panic at the approach of a stranger with a gun than at the approach of Mama with the curling iron. More passion is destroyed at the breakfast table than in a time warp.

Let's say you write a scene in which a young mother is taking a walk with her three-year-old daughter, whom she loves with every iota of her being. And let's say you have the little girl release Mommy's hand and dart between two parked cars out into the street, where she's hit by an oncoming bus. A melodramatic scene would have the mother running to the little girl, prostrating herself over the dead child's body while shrieking, gnashing her teeth, weeping copiously, shaking her fist at the heavens, cursing an unjust God, and beating her breast until she breaks ribs. Over the top. Like, *way* over the top! A more dramatic scene would instead have the mother simply slump to the curb, all the bones melting in her body, and take on that thousand-yard-stare that soldiers who've just been in heavy and intense combat sometimes have.

Instead of elevating the emotional language, the smart writer *flattens* it. As Toni Morrison said, "If the character cries on the page … the reader won't."

Look to poetry, look to music, look to movies, look to life—look everywhere a form of communication exists—for how to create dramatic scenes instead of melodramatic scenes. Look at nature. Look at the documentary on the Discovery Channel for the scene when the female lion cuts the tiny, weak wildebeest fawn out of the herd and brings her down by her neck while the mother looks on. See the sorrow and even the anger in the wildebeest mother as she helplessly watches her baby die, and you will see that Nature herself flattens the response, and that makes it even more powerful. It's the wildebeest's *actions*—understated, yet all the more powerful because of that—that evoke the emotion in the witness to the tragedy. As should the actions in your own scene.

Lower the volume; don't turn it up.

A marvelous example of opening a story with a truly dramatic (versus melodramatic) inciting incident can be seen in the movie *Thelma & Louise*. (This is Thelma's story, no matter the equal billing in the title.) The story opens with a series of very brief vignettes back and forth between the two women, establishing their relationship to each other and letting the audience know about a trip they're planning to take together. The inciting incident occurs right after, when Thelma is talking with her husband, Darryl, in the kitchen.

It quickly becomes obvious from Thelma and Darryl's conversation that Darryl is mostly condescending to his wife and has an exalted opinion of himself as being much smarter than Thelma. It's also clear he fancies himself a ladies' man and has been treating his wife badly for quite some time.

Thelma is on the verge of telling him about her impending trip with Louise and asking his permission to go, when he answers her innocuous and sweet, "Hon?" with a snide, impatient, "What," delivered in the tone of a parent condescending to a bothersome child. As a result of his tone, she decides to go without asking permission. This is a small but significant turning point—the inciting incident that creates the surface problem and starts to expose Thelma's deeply psychological story-worthy problem to both herself and viewers. This is a huge step for Thelma to take. She's never openly defied her husband before this moment. We don't know that explicitly—there's no setup or backstory provided by screenwriter Callie Khouri—but we grasp all of this through the context of their conversations and through

Chapter Three

glimpses into the circumstances of their marriage. This screenplay represents writing of the highest order and worthy of your study.

Now let's break this down a little further. In deciding not to ask Darryl's permission, Thelma takes her very first action to resolve her story-worthy problem (her domination by men). Even though she takes this first action, it's important to note that she doesn't fully realize the scope of her story-worthy problem. At this point, she sees her problem as limited to Darryl, when in actuality her story-worthy problem is that she allows *all* men to dominate and take advantage of her.

Her decision to go on the trip without asking permission is just her first step toward that realization—her eyes open the tiniest bit for the first time, even if she can't articulate it at that point. Everything that happens from then on in the story is a direct and causal result of that first action, this first glimmer of realization. After all, if she had asked for permission as she would have in the past, she most likely wouldn't have been allowed to go on the trip—a command she would have obeyed. Therefore, she wouldn't have made the second decision to beg Louise to stop at the roadhouse. And therefore she wouldn't have thrown caution to the wind and flirted and danced with Harlan. All these seemingly insignificant decisions set the stage for the initial surface problem when Harlan tries to rape Thelma, and Louise shoots him. Now we've got *trouble*. Everything that happens can be traced back to Darryl's tone and Thelma's decision to go on the trip without asking permission.

Note, too, how Khouri keeps the inciting incident from tipping into the melodramatic. A less-talented writer might have begun with the melodramatic parking lot scene where Louise plugs the bad guy (which is easily misinterpreted as the inciting incident), but Khouri chooses to begin with the true inciting (and dramatic) scene in the kitchen with Thelma subconsciously taking her first action to resolve her story-worthy problem. And her defiance isn't played out with heavy-handed melodrama. Khouri could have opened that scene by showing Darryl being abusive toward Louise, maybe having a knock-down argument or something mundane like that. All well and good, but if that's all the opening scene accomplished, then it wouldn't qualify as a proper opening. All such a scene would amount to would be backstory or setup. Instead, Khouri employs a more subtle approach. Thelma doesn't begin to scream at him or anything like that. It's a small action, but a dramatic one. She simply decides not to tell him about her plans with Louise and, more importantly, not to ask his permission to go. Pure drama. Of course, melodrama does come later in the movie when Louise shoots and kills the would-be rapist Harlan—after all, it's a *movie*, right?—but not at the onset.

Work on creating dramatic scenes instead of melodramatic scenes. Think smaller, not bigger. If you begin with a bombing, how are you going to top that? By subsequent bombings that get bigger and bigger and kill more and more people until you work up to nuclear explosions? Bad idea. Begin with a small moment of intense realization that affects your protagonist on an internal psychological level, and you have room to allow the problem to grow.

The Difference Between an Inciting Incident and a Situation

The mistake many writers make is confusing a *situation*—most times, a negative situation—with an inciting incident. A situation, according to *Merriam-Webster* anyway, is a "position with respect to conditions and circumstances." An inciting incident is the event that upsets the situation and pushes it to its breaking point.

Think about *Thelma & Louise* again. Prior to her small act of defiance, Thelma is more or less aware that she's involved in a bad relationship, but, as we come to learn during the remainder of the movie, she's been in a state of denial for most of her marriage. This means that for most of her marriage—for most of her story—she's lived within the confines of her circumstances, thus existing in a bad *situation*. Thelma's small act of defiance—her decision to finally *take action* and go on the trip with Louise without asking her husband for permission—is what turns her situation into a story. It is the event that creates the initial surface problem and sets up the introduction of the story-worthy problem.

Hooked

THE INCITING
INCIDENT AS A TRIGGER

As we've discussed, the inciting incident is the crucial event—the trouble—that sets the whole story in motion. It triggers the initial surface problem and starts to slowly expose the protagonist's story-worthy problem. Now, the protagonist won't fully realize the extent of his story-worthy problem in the opening scene, so the initial surface problem has to be so compelling that it forces him to take immediate action. The protagonist's understanding of his story-worthy problem, then, will grow clearer to him as a direct result of what he goes through in his journey to resolve it.

Also keep in mind that each of the protagonist's attempts to resolve the initial and subsequent surface problems must end in failure. There can be partial victories, but once an action ends in success, the story is effectively over. *Success*, in this case, means that all the problems are resolved. That cannot happen until the final scene of the story.

So, if we were to broadly outline the shape of a publishable story—the inciting incident and all its intertwined surface and story-worthy problems—it would look something like this:

- The inciting incident creates the character's initial surface problem and introduces the first inklings of the story-worthy problem.

- The protagonist takes steps to resolve the initial surface problem.

- The outcome of the major action the protagonist takes to resolve the initial surface problem is revealed, triggering a new surface problem. The scope of the protagonist's story-worthy problem continues to unfold.

- The outcome of the major action the protagonist takes to resolve the additional surface problem is revealed, and yet another surface problem is created. The story-worthy problem continues to become more apparent to the protagonist, as well as to the reader.

- Another outcome is revealed, and more surface problems are created. The story-worthy problem continues to become clearer.

- All lingering surface problems are resolved, and the story-worthy problem is fully realized. The resolution of the story-worthy problem is represented by both a win and a loss for the protagonist.

Notice that this isn't a point-by-point outline of a plot. Also, it isn't like an essay outline, in which you provide the nature of the actions to be taken (that "topic sentence" thing), but rather, the *outcome* of those actions. Further, take note of the fact that this kind of outline provides only for the *major* actions (of which there are usually three) the protagonist will take to resolve the problem. That leaves room for dozens (hundreds?) of other, smaller actions he can take to achieve his goal. This outline also leaves plenty of leeway for you, as the author, to choose what actions your protagonist will take, thus allowing you the artistic freedom to get the protagonist to the outcome any way the author wants to. In short, it provides a roadmap of highways for the narrative car, but it doesn't include the scenic routes.

An example of an inciting incident that kick-starts a novel is the one Scott Smith provided in his best-selling novel *A Simple Plan*, which was made into a film of the same name.

The story begins with a bit of necessary setup, giving a scrap of family history. The backstory is that the two chief characters in the story—Hank, the first-person narrator/protagonist, and his brother/antagonist, Jacob—never have anything to do with each other except once a year, when they visit their parents' graves together. The backstory also describes their parents' death in a car accident that was really a joint suicide. In this case, the backstory is crucial because it gives a plausible reason for Hank and Jacob to be together when the inciting incident occurs. It also works because it shows the reader the brothers' relationship to each other, and that relationship is Hank's story-worthy problem. This is a Cain-and-Abel story, and therefore the brothers' history is important to the reader's understanding of what's about to transpire. The entire history takes a little less than three pages to detail before the narrative enters the inciting incident scene. Jacob, accompanied by his dog, Mary Beth, and by their friend Lou, picks up Hank for their annual pilgrimage. During the trip to the gravesite, a fox runs across the icy road. Jacob has a slight accident, and Mary Beth takes off after the fox. The three men go after the dog and discover a plane downed in a field. In the plane, they discover a dead pilot and a bag filled with three million dollars, and they figure out it's probably drug money.

The initial surface problem begins with this discovery. Hank, the straight-arrow brother with the pregnant wife, college degree, and professional job, wants to do the right thing and turn in the money, but Jacob, who's a ne'er-do-well, high school dropout alcoholic, and Lou talk him out of it. Against his better judgment, Hank accedes, and the brothers plunge into a spiral of darkness until they get to the place where Hank kills his brother.

Finding the money and the decision that the discovery forces Hank to make is the inciting incident, and it is delivered via a scene so that the reader experiences what Hank does, at the same time he does it; the reader experiences the same dilemma he does, emotionally. Hank's surface problem is how to please his brother by keeping the money, while assuaging his conscience at the same time. Plus, he needs to avoid discovery of their crime and keep from going to jail and ruining his life. His story-worthy problem—his lifelong guilt over his good fortune in life and his brother's wasted existence—(which is tied directly to the surface problem) has been forced to the surface by their parents' deaths, which is why the brief backstory at the start of this story works.

The protagonist's action in agreeing to split up the money instead of turning it in—an action he takes in order to gain his brother's love—is a flawed action, just as was Thelma's in agreeing with Louise to not turn themselves in after Louise kills Harlan. In each of these two stories, both instances of well-meant-but-flawed actions by the protagonist are responsible for the surface problem and are similar in nature. And, in both instances, the surface problem exists to serve as the vehicle that drives the story-worthy problem along the journey.

Harlan Coben's novel *No Second Chance* begins with a compelling first sentence:

> When the first bullet hit my chest, I thought of my daughter.

The protagonist awakens in a hospital bed to discover his daughter has been kidnapped and his wife slain. His story-worthy problem—guilt over not protecting his wife and child—is tied to the initial surface problem—to get his daughter back safe. Both problems hatch from the same egg, as do the protagonist's goals:

to get his daughter back, and to regain his self-respect as a protective and caring father.

STORY-WORTHY PROBLEMS VS. SURFACE PROBLEMS

Many writers confuse their initial surface problem with their a story-worthy problem. What's the difference? A lot, as it turns out. As we discussed at the start of this chapter, a story-worthy problem always relates more to the inner psychology of the protagonist and has to be big enough, dramatic enough, to change the protagonist's world and force him on a journey of change. Surface problems, on the other hand, are more like bad situations that reflect the actual story-worthy problem, but that aren't sufficient on their own to sustain an entire story.

As the author, you should have a firm understanding of your story-worthy problem before you begin writing. This will help you to provide your protagonist with an initial surface problem that kicks off the action of the story and successfully draws out your intended story-worthy problem. Remember that since your story-worthy problem is always a deeper psychological problem, it won't be completely understood by your protagonist—or by your reader—until the end of the story (we'll discuss this in greater detail on page 71), but you'll need to know what exactly what the problem is from page 1 in order to make sure all your story's problems are linked.

Every problem—story-worthy and surface—has its own corresponding resolution or goal, so the resolution of a surface problem shouldn't also be the resolution to the story-worthy problem. Instead, the resolution of the surface problem should *contribute* to the resolution of the story-worthy problem. They are, after all, as closely related as peanut butter and jelly.

You have to dig deep to find your real story problem. And if you don't do the work of figuring out your character's story-worthy problem before beginning your story, you stand a good chance of ending up with a story that's too slight or superficial. For instance, there are all kinds of problems in real life that make our lives ratty and even nasty. Poverty, the death or disappearance of a loved one, an unexpected visit from the IRS, whatever. But, unless there's something more, something deeper at stake than a mere reversal of fortune, you're going to end up with a weak story. Sure, those problems are bad, but in fiction they merely represent surface problems and by themselves can't achieve the depth needed to qualify as a good story problem.

CREATING YOUR STORY'S PROBLEMS AND GOALS

How do you get from a surface problem to a story-worthy problem? One way is to keep asking yourself *Why?* questions. For instance, let's say you've dreamed up a story about a protagonist named Sydney who you want to take through all kinds of adventures and travails as he hunts for the lost city of Xenon. You might ask yourself at this point, "*Why* does my character want to find this city?" The quick and easy answer might be something like, "He wants to be lionized in archaeological circles for the find of a lifetime." Or, "He wants to gain fame and fortune." Another answer might be, "The beautiful Lolita (the love of his life) sees Sydney as sweet but weak and unable to defend himself. He wants to win her heart by showing her his bravery and resourcefulness." His surface problem is he doesn't have fame or fortune or recognition or love. His surface goal is to find the lost city, which will give him that fame, fortune, recognition, or love.

These are all superficial, overt goals representing superficial rewards. To uncover the story-worthy problem, look deeper into your own heart and the heart of your character. Our character's desires are really our own, you know. Ask yourself what Sydney *really* wants to gain. Well, you might say, he wants to gain the lovely Lolita's hand, and finding the lost city would impress her enough to achieve that goal. Now you're getting somewhere. Let's keep going.

Play devil's advocate for a minute. Ask yourself if Sydney couldn't gain Lolita's love with a less risky course of action. Well … maybe. But, there's that Walter thing. … A year before, when Sydney first fell in love with Lolita and it looked as if she was falling for him as well, along came Walter, who made Sydney eat sand. In front of Lolita! He didn't even try to defend himself that day because he was afraid of Walter. Ever since then, she's been nice to him—*overly* nice, in fact—but he can tell it's pity he's getting from her now. He knows in his heart of hearts that feeling sorry for someone isn't going to translate into love. At least, not *adult* love.

By the way, this Walter thing is probably your inciting incident and where the story should begin. The day Walter embarrassed him, Sydney's story-worthy problem was introduced when he lost Lolita's respect. But to make this work as the inciting incident, you'll have to change the time frame a bit. You can't have Sydney taking his first action a year after his problem has been revealed to him. If that amount of time can transpire before Sydney takes action, then it wasn't really a story-worthy problem. Remember, once the story-worthy problem is introduced, nothing can take precedence over it. In this case, it's easily fixed. Just begin with the scene where Walter makes Sydney eat sand, and immediately have Sydney take his first step to resolve the problem. Or, you can account for a year's time by having Sydney's first action to resolve the problem last that long. For instance, you could speed through that year by including a sentence like: "After that day at the beach, Sydney dove into the bottom of a bottle—rather a long series of bottles—for the better part of a year."

63 ⌀

All of this means that Sydney really isn't after the lost city of Xenon. He's really after Lolita. Only it turns out he's really after something even larger and more important than Lolita. He needs to gain his own self-respect. He needs to prove he isn't a coward. For Lolita and even more for himself. His entire sense of self is tied to his one cowardly act. Lolita just represents what he lost when he lost his self-respect.

Now you're *really* getting somewhere! You're thinking like a writer. You've finally gotten down to that dark place we all have inside and fight the hardest to ignore and deny. The place where all good story problems reside. You've done it—you've figured out what Sydney's true story-worthy problem is. Finding the lost city was only the surface problem and surface goal. Sydney's story-worthy problem and story-worthy goal was to find himself, although he won't be aware of that until the final scene—the resolution. In his own mind, his problem is finding the lost city, his goal the reward he'll get when he finds it (Lolita's love). It's only during the final scene of the story that he gains insight into what he was really after—self-respect; that what he wanted all along wasn't really Lolita's love, but what that love represented to his sense of self. It is also very possible that he may realize that he doesn't need another person's love to gain that self-respect.

This is how the surface problems and goals relate to the story-worthy problem and goal. If you stop at only providing your character surface problems and surface goals, then you don't have a story, at least not a quality story. You must go deeper.

If you have trouble distinguishing between your surface problem goals and story-worthy problem goals, here's an easy way to remember the difference (this may also help you to write better scenes centered around surface problems and goals): You should be able to photograph the resolution of a surface problem. For instance, let's say a character's story-worthy goal is to win the love of a fair damsel, who represents the recovery of self-esteem for that character. Now love isn't a goal that can be photographed. But, if the character equates making physical love with the object of his affection as representative of the concept of love, then that (having sex) can be photographed. Surface goals are particular, while story-worthy goals are all-encompassing and more general. World peace cannot be photographed, but a truce with a combative neighbor can be (as represented by shaking hands or hugging).

You can use this concept in a practical way. When you begin to write a scene in which the protagonist is struggling to achieve a surface goal, picture the goal he's after in a single photograph. This will help you tremendously in focusing and tightening the scene.

Also, remember to keep asking yourself what it is that your character really wants—what his real problem is. Your protagonist's story-worthy goal is probably very close to a goal you want to achieve for yourself. The truth is, writing of any sort can be cathartic; it can help the author discover a hard truth about himself. A truth he perhaps wasn't even aware of when he began on page 1. If a story only catalogues a series of disasters without putting them into context, the writing will be neither cathartic nor healing. It'll simply be a superficial story. Journalism, not fiction (and bad journalism at that).

If you approach your fiction story as merely a series of events—if you simply have your character go through a struggle to achieve a lost city—all you'll have is a superficial story. Same o', same o'.

What transforms a story is the inner psychological problem of the protagonist being laid bare on the page.

But, guess what: *You've* got it! You've figured out what your character really wants and what's truly at stake for him. Once you've figured that out, it's time to begin writing. You've just done a lot of the heavy lifting.

Let One Lead to the Other: The Interconnectedness of a Story's Problems and Goals

A protagonist's problems—both of the surface and storyworthy variety—must lead directly to the establishment of corresponding goals. The goal of the protagonist, of course, is to resolve his problems. For instance, once the initial surface problem is introduced into the story, the protagonist begins to take action to resolve it. As that takes place, the problem becomes worse and the obstacles more and more difficult. If the protagonist only resolves a portion of the initial surface problem, then another problem comes forth, and so on. This continues until the final scene, at which point not only are the surface problems resolved, but the *real* (story-worthy) problem is at last fully revealed and resolved. Let's study closely how that sequence of problem/resolution takes place by looking again at *Thelma & Louise*.

The first surface problem occurs when Louise shoots and kills Thelma's attacker, Harlan. This is the crucial surface problem that provides the narrative thrust and propels the plot along. Make sure that your initial surface problem arises from the story-worthy problem. It has to be organic and not just come out of nowhere.

As we discussed earlier, *Thelma & Louise* opens with a display of the story-worthy problem (Thelma's domination by Darryl), which leads to the melodramatic initial surface problem when Louise shoots Harlan. The surface problem is obvious—Thelma and Louise must now run from the law to escape imprisonment or execution.

If Thelma hadn't realized she was under Darryl's domination (and, by inference, men in general), she probably would have persisted in trying to convince Louise to surrender to the police and tell their side of the story. It's because she's finally aware that women don't have a chance in a male-dominated world (and because she is struggling to resolve her story-worthy problem) that she doesn't persist in convincing Louise to surrender. And the chase is on. On the surface and entertainment levels, avoiding capture is the goal, but Thelma's real and more important goal is achieving her independence from men.

By connecting the story-worthy problem to a strong first surface problem, you'll create a story that barrels along on two levels—your protagonist striving to resolve the surface problem as well as the deeper story-worthy problem. The surface problem is a means of portraying the more significant story-worthy problem and is representative of it. If you were to neglect providing a surface problem and instead simply focus on the internal, psychological problem, you'd have a story mostly containing the character's ruminations. The surface problem provides the vehicle that will carry the story-worthy problem along and keep the reader interested and involved.

By the same token, if *Thelma & Louise* had only been about the surface problem—the women running from the law—it would never have achieved the resonance and literary merit it did with the deeper, psychological story of escaping male dominance. If this had been a novel instead of a film, and had only contained the surface problem—escaping the law and imprisonment or death— it might have enjoyed a brief success, but it would surely have been consigned to the annual garage sale as soon as it was read. With the deeper, interior, story-worthy problem that the film embraced, it would have remained on the owner's shelf to be reread again and again.

When you're writing your own story, it's crucial that you remember to give your antagonist an equally relevant goal. His goal has to conflict with the protagonist's goal. That's where the conflict and tension in the story mainly comes from. Try not to make your antagonist's goals evil. Do that and you'll create Snidely Whiplash. The best stories are tales in which both the protagonist's and the antagonist's goals are equally good and honorable. In *Thelma & Louise*, Thelma's antagonist in the surface problem is Hal, the detective who's after the two women. Hal's goals are totally honorable; his motive is twofold: First, he believes in upholding the law as he's sworn to do; and second, he simply wants to capture the girls before they're killed. His goal is in complete opposition to Thelma's, which is to remain free. If Hal were simply a guy who hated all criminals and especially these two women, then he'd be a Snidely Whiplash cartoon character. Bad guy vs. good gal. Not compelling.

HOW MANY PROBLEMS SHOULD YOUR NOVEL CONTAIN?

The short answer is one story-worthy problem and innumerable surface problems.

The long answer is the same.

Surface problems are basically the author's way of representing the story-worthy problem in a dramatic way. As you've seen, they represent the underlying, much more intense and psychological story-worthy problem that's at the core of every story. And from that central problem a number of surface problems can and should develop.

Back to our example of *Thelma & Louise*. Thelma's story-worthy problem is she's lived most of her life under the dominance of males (specifically, her husband, Darryl). Her first overt goal is to achieve her independence from Darryl by going on a trip with Louise and having some fun at a roadhouse. After Louise shoots and kills Harlan, and the resultant surface problem (their pursuit by the law) is set in motion, Thelma begins to gain a broader understanding of the real story-worthy problem; the ensuing chase magnifies her struggle in a male-dominated world. Her overt goal for independence from Darryl and her story-worthy goal for independence from all men are tied directly to and emanate from her initial surface problem and her story-worthy problem. The story-worthy problem and the surface problem have a cause-and-effect relationship.

Thelma's surface problems change in virtually every scene. However, every single one of those problems is connected to her story-worthy problem. Her first problem is how to take the vacation with Louise, over the anticipated refusal of her husband to allow her to go. Then, she has a *big* problem when Louise shoots and kills Harlan. She needs to decide whether to flee the scene to avoid capture and imprisonment. Every new surface problem arises out of the last problem.

YOUR CHARACTER'S AWARENESS OF HIS OWN STORY-WORTHY PROBLEM

Your story begins with the inciting incident, which creates the protagonist's initial surface problem and sets up the story-worthy problem. Right, you know this already. But here's where things get a little tricky: Your protagonist isn't going to recognize what his story-worthy problem or story-worthy goal is when he begins his journey. In fact, he can't at that point. He'll *think* he does and wholeheartedly believe he does, but at the beginning he really doesn't. He may even sense the real problem, but he won't know for sure what it is until he goes through the struggle to resolve the related surface problems. It's the course of that struggle and what he learns during it that will deliver to him what he's really been after and what his real problem is. The reader won't know what the protagonist's true story-worthy problem is at the beginning of the story, either. Rather, the reader will realize it at the same time the protagonist does. As the character progresses through his struggle, he'll begin to come closer and closer to the truth of his search. As will the reader. You need to have him go through that struggle to find that out, though.

Of course, while readers and your character may not be fully aware of the story-worthy problem at the start of the story, it is crucial that *you*, as the creator of this guy and his story, do know what his real problem is.

Only if you know his real story-worthy problem before you begin writing can you create the kind of story that will reveal that problem to your character. Makes sense, doesn't it? And even though the protagonist doesn't yet fully understand his problem, he should have a deep sense of it, a sense he won't be able to articulate or understand until he actually goes through the struggle. Make no mistake: The story-worthy problem is always there—it just takes time (and struggle) to reveal it fully to both the character and reader.

Before you begin it's also imperative that you know what your protagonist's initial surface problem is and how it supports the story-worthy problem, because unless you do, how on earth are you going to come up with the right story opening? You really can't. After all, the initial surface problem is what gets your character going, since he truly believes it to be his real problem. Remember, he doesn't yet realize the nature of his story-worthy problem, so without the initial surface problem he'd have no reason to begin his journey.

Full understanding only comes with the resolution itself. That's what the resolution is all about—an insight gained into the character's problem as a result of his struggle and the answer to that problem. It's his moment of total awareness. The character senses, on some level, what his story-worthy problem might be right from the start, after the inciting incident. However, the problem won't be fully formed in his mind at that point. It will become clearer and clearer to him as he goes through his struggle, bit by bit, revelation by revelation. This is a difficult concept to master and difficult to carry through in the writing of a story, but it is absolutely necessary to understand.

Let me see if I can make it clearer. In my short story "My Idea of a Nice Thing," the inciting incident occurs for the protagonist, Raye, when she "hits her bottom," evidenced by her not being able to go to sleep with her old trick of picturing goldfish. She's been an alcoholic for a long time and was vaguely aware of her situation, but until she hit her bottom she didn't realize the severity of her problem. Her story-worthy problem is that she's unable to reconcile being the sober and healthy person society demands with her deep wish to remain an artist (she plays the cornet). It's the reason she vacillates between sobriety and binges. Her story-worthy problem is introduced on the first page when she addresses an A.A. meeting by saying:

> "It's why I drink," she said, the first time she stood up at A.A. "My job. I'm a hairdresser. See, you take on all of these other people's personalities and troubles and things, ten or twelve of 'em a day, and when the end of the day comes, you don't know who *you* are."

Her words indicate she's acutely aware she has a problem, but the true nature of her problem and its scope aren't yet fully revealed to her. As her struggle continues, it will become clearer to her what her problem really is, and at the resolution she'll realize it wasn't alcoholism itself that was the problem, but rather her inability to operate in the world as a sober person and retain her artistic soul that depended on alcohol. Her resolution is a true resolution in that it represents both a win and a loss. She chooses art over life.

INNER DEMONS: MINING FOR STORY-WORTHY PROBLEMS

The best sources for significant story problems reside within yourself in the form of your personal demons. The very best writers are those who are courageous enough to go deep inside themselves to face and expose the warts and hidden desires and forbidden feelings most of us want to hide from or deny, at least to others. Not everyone is able to face his demons and bring them out to the light of day, but if you have a fear, a forbidden thought or yearning, or an experience that has scarred or deeply affected you, then you have the material of great literature and of great story problems. For one thing, you are dealing with material that is powerfully emotional to you already. And emotion is the chief coin in the trade of writers. It's what we strive most to elicit from our readers. Therefore, if we bring intense emotion to the writing of the story, our chances of obtaining a strong emotional response from readers is virtually assured.

Of course, what people really want—both in fiction and in real life—when a significant problem arises, is for the problem to have never happened in the first place. This is our true goal. To figure out a way to turn back time, to make it so the disaster never occurred. Think about your own life. Perhaps you were cheated on by someone you loved desperately. Wasn't your first thought that you wished it was still last Thursday, the day before you learned of his infidelity? Wasn't your second thought that you wished you'd never found out?

Well, even though that is our real goal, it's an impossible goal. It *did* happen, and no one has yet figured out a way to turn back time and change events. Interestingly, that's the reason there have been so many books, plays, movies, and stories about time travel. Those stories are hugely popular and have been ever since we began to communicate our feelings to each other. We all wish we could turn back the pages of time and reverse our bad fortune.

You can't have your characters using the space of your story or book to wish for the impossible any more than you can function in the real world by spending all your time wishing you could go back and rewrite history. But, if you as the creator of a fictional world realize that this is the real wish of your character, you'll have a better understanding of human nature and, therefore, your character.

Since the real goal to return to the world that existed before the problem arrived is impossible, the next best goal is to return as close to possible to that world.

Essentially, a world minus the problem. That's the reason many of a person's actions, both in fiction and in life, are designed to make the person he views as responsible for his predicament change his mind. A jilted lover, for instance, flaunts a new boyfriend in front of the old lover in an attempt to make him feel jealous and sorry for his loss, and to convince him to take her back (and restore the old world order).

Smaller and Particular Works;
Grandiose and Immense Doesn't Work

Good and worthy story problems derive from the small and the particular and the individual. Not the grandiose. Don't begin a story with the intent of writing about a grand topic, such as freedom, for instance. To run with that example and clarify it a bit, some years ago we had civil strife in this country over states' rights versus federalism and slavery, among other things. We called it the Civil War. I wasn't there, although my kids seem to think that I was, but I do know that there were a great many essays and speeches written on both sides about the conflict—even without chat rooms—and that most of those are now forgotten except to academics specializing in such knowledge.

What lots more people do remember about this chapter in our history, however, is a little book titled *Uncle Tom's Cabin*, written by a lady named Harriet Beecher Stowe. This book had a powerful effect on the nation, both the North and the South. Why? Because she focused on one particular, the life of Uncle Tom and the effect of slavery upon him. If she'd instead opted to write some sweeping polemic about the evils of slavery, it's doubtful many would remember it today or that they even would have read it at the time she wrote it.

As an example of how important it is to forget big, lofty themes in favor of small individual examples, I ask the students in my classes how many of their parents, to get them to eat their vegetables when they were tadpoles, trotted out variations of that dinosaur saying almost all parents have used forever: "Eat your spinach, Oscar. There are eighty kazillion starving people in China that would love to have what you're wasting." (This was before China became a major economic force on the world financial stage.)

Just about all the students hold up their hands.

"Did it make you eat your spinach?" I ask.

Nope, they reply.

"Now," I say, "what if your dad or mom had said, 'Junior, eat all of your peas. Old Lady Smithers, who lives two doors down, has lost her job and her unemployment just ran out. Just last night, I caught her going through our garbage can looking for scraps of bread. *She'd* sure like those peas!'"

I'd like to report that I get unanimous agreement that this specific example would have gotten the kids to eat their peas, but alas, I don't. I do get about half the class to admit that, yes, they might eat their peas with the second example, and I'm grateful for that.

The point is, "eighty kazillion starving Chinese people" is a faceless problem. It's meaningless. We don't see anyone. On the other hand, we get a clear picture of Old Lady Smithers digging about in our garbage can for scraps. That gives us an emotional connection and drives the point home much more forcibly.

Do the same with your story problems. Don't make your character's problem World Peace. Instead, give us a story about war-weary Arnold Smathers, who struggles to make friends with his nasty and overbearing neighbor, Big Bing Binglerschmidt. Let Arnie perform those actions in the course of his struggle that will bring peace to Arnie at least, and perhaps even the entire neighborhood.

Always get your story down to the level of individuals. We can see individuals. We can't see The Forces of Capitalism vs. The Forces of Communism.

CHAPTER FOUR

The Setup and Backstory

Now that you understand how inciting incidents and story-worthy and surface problems function and why they're so essential to an opening scene, let's look at how to correctly use setup and backstory to add texture to the story problem and to magnify the importance of the inciting incident.

Of the ten components of an opening scene (as delineated on pages 24 through 36 of chapter two), setup and backstory are of such importance that I'm devoting a full chapter to them here, immediately after our discussion of the inciting incident, story-worthy problem, and initial surface problem. You may be asking yourself why, if backstory is so important, did I list it as a secondary component instead of a primary one. Fair question. I listed it as a secondary component to make sure you wouldn't be tempted to overuse it in your opening, not to marginalize its relevancy when used correctly. Backstory is incorrectly included in the setup so often that I felt it would be beneficial to discuss them together in this chapter. It's just as crucial to discuss what *shouldn't* be incorporated in an opening—especially when it's so commonly done—as it is to talk about what should be included, and that's what we're going to look at now.

The most common *wrong* opening is beginning your story with too much setup or backstory. This isn't to say that there isn't a place for the setup or backstory in the beginning; this is to say that most writers simply put too much of it in the wrong place. Setup and backstory can come later in the opening chapter or later in the novel, just not at the very beginning, in most cases.

The incorrect placement of backstory stems from the mistaken belief that readers won't know what's going on unless the author fleshes out the characters or provides some of the protagonist's history and at least part of the journey that brought the protagonist to this crucial place.

This is the single biggest mistake writers make.

A setup that very (very!) briefly lets readers know who the characters are and where they are is usually fine; a setup that includes excruciating minutiae of a long backstory usually isn't. Give only the amount of setup or backstory that's absolutely necessary, and not a word more. More often than not, no backstory is even needed. Try to create setups that include necessary backstory concisely, and trust the reader to get what's going on.

For example, you could begin a story by writing:

The man had a reputation around town for being a brawler and a mean-spirited drunk. Ever since high school, when he had bullied just about every kid littler than him, he'd been known as a person to avoid. See him coming and walk across the street to avoid passing by at close quarters. It might have been his parents who created his personality. Most likely his father, who was known as the town drunk—at least on the northeast side of Fort Wayne—who spent a lot of time whaling on his son with whatever he found handy. A belt, a stick, whatever was available. One time he clopped him upside the head with an iron he snatched off the ironing board behind which his mother stood, helplessly wringing her hands. It might have been the dead-end factory job he'd found himself stuck in for the past thirty-two years.

His marriage of the past twenty-eight years didn't seem to have had much of a positive effect on his personality either. Nobody had noticed much of a change from the dour, nasty face he presented to the world each morning when he left his house for work, cursing out loud most of those mornings at finding the morning newspaper too far from his front door for his taste. Most of the neighbors wondered why she hadn't left him a long time ago. Especially since she'd been miserable with the cancer for the past two years. Why, everyone wondered, would anyone dying keep on subjecting herself to the misery that was her husband, in addition to her painful affliction. Just this past evening, in fact, she'd screamed for over an hour when the pain pills the doctor had given her had again failed to do the trick, and the neighbors on both sides had heard the noise.

She *had* left him, although the neighbors didn't know it. She'd left everybody. She was dead. At this moment, he found himself about six blocks from his home with his dead bride in his arms. On State Street just past Maplecrest, in the Georgetown Shopping Plaza. Behind it, actually, back by the dumpsters behind the Cap 'N Cork.

You *could* begin a story that way—with all the backstory this opening provides. Or you could begin this way:

He was so mean that wherever he was standing became the bad part of town.

At that moment, the bad part was State Street just past Maplecrest, in the Georgetown Shopping Plaza. Behind it, actually, back by the dumpsters behind the Cap 'N Cork.

Into one of which he was stuffing the body of his wife.

There's some setup in the second version, and some backstory, but it's brief and it's all the reader needs to understand the story (my short story, "The Bad Part of Town"). The same backstory that appears in the first version does appear in the second version, but later in the story. Where it belongs.

If you've got a story you want to write and simply can't get over the urge to begin with a lot of setup or backstory, then you need to step back and rethink your story.

You might find that you're trying to start the story in the wrong place. If this is the case, perhaps you need to begin your story further back than you imagined, rather than provide backstory to set up what happens. Or, better, just include most of that backstory (if it's truly important) later on in the story.

Let's take a closer look first at setup, then at backstory, and then at how to correctly balance the two elements in an opening.

THE SETUP

The setup is just that—setting up the situation, or characters, or both. Most of the time, at least some backstory is included in the setup. In fact, the terms are somewhat interchangeable, and this is why they're often paired. When backstory is used to preface the inciting incident, it becomes a major element of the setup.

The setup can also be employed with very little backstory. It may consist simply of introducing a character with a brief synopsis of her situation. A story may begin with the author showing the restaurant her two main characters are eating dinner in, and plunge right into the inciting incident. Using the setup like that is perfectly okay. Just don't overdo it. If you describe the restaurant in minute detail, itemize the two characters' menu choices, provide a full description of the waiter, discuss a hurricane a hundred miles north of them that is blowing toward the restaurant, and reveal the protagonist's earlier encounter with a hurricane, then you're probably including too much setup. A wee bit of setup is fine—after all, it's important to ground the characters physically in the reader's mind before the action begins—but the key is to choose your words wisely and to be succinct.

Make sure that the setup includes only the bare minimum necessary to make the story work, and make sure it's written with skill. Keep in mind that almost all stories have at least some setup at the beginning, even if it's just a few words, like "Rose Marie found herself stranded on the top of a mountain in the Urals when ..." If, in one or two sentences before the inciting incident occurs, you show readers that your characters are a man and a woman, and that they're having coffee at an outdoor café, technically, you've written a setup. As we've already discussed, one difference between today's stories and those of yesteryear is that, in the majority of today's stories, setup has to be minimal and very brief. No long descriptions of the characters and their relationships and past histories and all that. In another era, that worked. No longer is that the case.

The best way to use setup is to incorporate it into the action of the inciting incident itself, as Charles Baxter does in the opening of his short story "Saul and Patsy Are Pregnant":

> A smell of spilled gasoline: when Saul opened his eyes, he was still strapped in behind his lap-and-shoulder

> belt, but the car he sat in was upside down and in a
> field of some sort.

We've been given just enough detail to know that an auto-mobile accident has just occurred in the country and Saul is trapped in his car and smells gasoline. We're plopped down immediately into the inciting incident, and we have a clear idea of where the character is and what's happening. Baxter doesn't give us any more than what is necessary, because he knows we, being the astute readers we are, will furnish the flesh for the skeleton shown on the page. For instance, he only says that Saul is in a field. He doesn't say what kind of field—is it a hay field, a wheat field, a corn field, a field of weeds? It doesn't matter—we'll furnish our own version, and whatever version that is will be correct. Myself, I saw a wheat field and a flat landscape stretching forever, prob-ably because I've lived in Indiana for several years and that's what I see every day. Am I right? Did Baxter visualize a field of sorghum or sugar beets or tobacco instead when he wrote this? It doesn't matter. The kind of field isn't important to this story—only the fact that it's a field and obviously in the country. From that tiny bit of setup integrated into the ac-tion of the event, we are smoothly immersed into the incit-ing incident and resultant story.

BACKSTORY

Backstory is essentially a character's history. What's gone on in your protagonist's and other characters' past inform what they do and what will happen in the present of the story. In other words, backstory encapsulates just about anything and everything that comes before the inciting incident in your story's timeline.

The key with backstory is determining where it should appear and how much of it is necessary for the reader's understanding and appreciation of the story. Of course backstory has a place in a story; in fact, without it, many times a story is incomplete. That instinct many writers have to provide detailed backstory isn't always misguided.

But (*big* but) it is often misplaced.

Backstory has its place in a story, but that place isn't *usually* at the very beginning (of course, there are exceptions, and we'll get to those shortly). At one time, yes, you could begin a story with backstory and get away with it. Not so much these days. The times have changed, and writing has changed significantly. Most of us no longer listen to disco music or wear bleeding madras shirts (oops, madras seems to be making a comeback), and most of us don't read stories that begin with the protagonist's complete history, up to the point when he realizes he's looking for love in all the wrong places.

As noted earlier, when backstory begins a story, it's also setup, because it's setting up prior events and leading into the present of the story—the inciting incident. But the setup doesn't always have to include backstory. Sometimes, the setup is merely letting the reader know there are two people in a room and they're doing something. None, or at least not much, of their personal history is involved. "Two men sit across a chessboard from each other in Trafalgar Square, and one turns to the other and says ..." That's setup, pure and simple, and there's nothing wrong with it. However, if the author details how one or both of those men happened to arrive at Trafalgar Square, especially with information such as "Charles's father paid a small fortune for acknowledged chess masters to teach him the game when he was a child ...," then the author has provided backstory as at least a portion of the setup.

As literary agent Jodie Rhodes advises, authors should "never open with long boring explanations of the protagonist's past." They should "[a]lways open with scenes that immediately engage us emotionally."

While Rhodes is right about not opening with backstory, she doesn't mean that backstory can't be in your opening at all. It just shouldn't be first. (Of course, there are exceptions to every rule, and I'll get to those in the next section.)

The key is this: Everything in moderation. First, think about the needs of your scene. What emotion are you going for? What does the reader absolutely need to know? What pace are you striving to establish? The odds are, you don't have to provide your protagonist's life history to achieve the scene's goals.

Take a gander at how writer Tim Sandlin begins his black-comedy road novel, *Sorrow Floats,* for a good example of how to weave in necessary backstory in the opening.

> My behavior slipped after Daddy died and went to San Francisco. I danced barefoot in bars, I flipped the bird at churches. Early one morning in April I drove Dothan's new pickup truck off the Snake River dike, and when the tow truck crew showed up they found me squatting on a snow patch in my nightgown crying over the body of a dead plover.

Again, as in all good writing, only the tip of the iceberg is revealed in this opening. Sandlin doesn't say a word about the depth of Maurey Talbot's relationship with her father, and he doesn't have to. Just showing Maurey's reaction to his death tells the reader plenty, and in a minimum of words.

Maurey's struggle to resolve her father's death truly begins when she drives over the dike and is discovered crying over the dead bird (the story's inciting incident). The rest of the history between her and her dad will be unveiled throughout the course of the novel, but we can already see by this opening that the relationship was crucial, and that it's the reason behind her story-worthy problem. How do we know this? Simple. Sandlin says so in the casual sentence, "My behavior slipped after Daddy died and went to San Francisco." Read: "My world began to change after Daddy died." Notice the use of *slipped*. That rather slight verb choice indicates that the narrator is not yet aware of the magnitude of her story-worthy problem (her inability to grow up, take control over her life, and stop acting like a little girl). But we, as readers, know we're in for one emotional ride. And, in just two sentences, Sandlin takes us from point A (when her father died) to point B (when Maurey's real inner journey begins).

A brief sidenote. The reason Maurey's father's death itself isn't the inciting incident goes back to our melodrama vs. drama discussion from chapter three. It is only when Maurey sees the dead bird that the initial surface problem is created and the story-worthy problem is really introduced. Not that she didn't have the story-worthy problem before; she did. But until that point Maurey was just a woman grieving for her father—a woman in a *bad situation*. I think the confusion comes about because we're used to noticing the "big" or "melodramatic" moments, but the moments that really count are the dramatic moments. Dad dying equals a melodramatic moment; the first small realization of just what that death really means to Maurey—which occurs when she sees the dead plover—equals dramatic moment.

Also, it's conceivably possible to argue that almost any event is an inciting incident, even the birth of a character (if the character wasn't born, then nothing would have happened, etc.), but a bad situation isn't an inciting incident. Until the creation of the initial surface problem, until the first inklings of the story-worthy problem are revealed to the character, your story hasn't started. Before Maurey sees that plover, sure, she's in a sad state, but it's still just a bad situation. *Bad in real life, but not bad enough for fiction.* She drinks and acts out, but until she sees the plover there are still other things that can occupy her thoughts and energy. After she begins to realize the depth of her problem, nothing takes precedence and that's what transforms her bad situation into a true inciting incident. (This is a tough, tough concept to grasp, and that's why we're revisiting it throughout this book.)

Maurey's situation before the inciting incident is very similar to Thelma's in *Thelma & Louise*. Thelma was emotionally abused by her husband probably for the whole of their married life, but she pretty much ignored it. Once she begins to acknowledge her story-worthy problem (her willingness to be dominated by men), the trouble starts and the story begins. Just as Thelma is moved to action by the tone of Darryl's voice when she is about to ask his permission, so is Sandlin's character awakened to her problem when she sees the plover. We need Maurey's brief history about the death of her father to make sense of what happens when she sees the bird, but that information is only backstory; it is not the inciting incident. We'll receive more necessary history at the proper time—later in the story. For now, it's enough to see her reaction. We'll fill in the reason for her reaction ourselves because Sandlin has trusted our intelligence to do so. It all comes back to trusting the reader.

When you read stories and novels, you are reading writing textbooks. Begin to look at fiction that way, and your writing will begin to improve by gargantuan leaps. When you read a novel you like, pay close attention to how the author began the story. If she began with backstory, was it delivered as a passive chunk of the character's history, or was it incorporated seamlessly into the present of a scene? Chances are, if you enjoyed the book, the writer did the latter.

Passive Backstory vs. Active Backstory

When the story material calls for at least some backstory, the proper way to include it is to introduce at least some of it *during* the inciting incident by weaving it in with the present action of the scene instead of placing it in a flashback. A crackerjack example of this is in Elmore Leonard's short story "Fire in the Hole."

> They had dug coal together as young men and then lost touch over the years. Now it looked like they'd be meeting again, this time as lawman and felon, Raylan Givens and Boyd Crowder.

An entire history between two men that speaks volumes. In two sentences, we learn they had a history from when they were young men (it's implied they're at least middle-aged now) and that they had both been employed as honest workmen at that time. Somewhere between those youthful years and the time of the story, they'd each traveled different paths—one pursued criminals, and the other became one. A lot of history preceding the inciting incident is included here, and it's short, sweet, and (most importantly) woven into the present of the story.

In fiction's days of yore, it was perfectly acceptable (and even encouraged) to craft great blocks of passive description, also referred to as windowpane description. This was the kind of description one might deliver while gazing out a window, and employed various poetic techniques. In one of those novels of yesteryear, readers were treated to blocks of prose describing a beach scene, for instance, in which paragraph after paragraph was employed to describe such things as "wind-burnished sands" and "skittering waves, rolling toward the breast-shaped hummocks of the sun-kissed beach." Yeah. Stuff like that. Such novels require the reader to plow through paragraph after paragraph of static descriptions.

Today, static (or passive) description is eschewed in favor of active description, description incorporated within the action of the scene itself: "As he raced onto Bryan Beach after the bad guy, moonlight glinted off a piece of broken glass." The reader furnishes the rest of the description from that one little item, and the action of the scene isn't stalled or even slowed down. Active versus passive description.

Perhaps we can even invent some new terms for the different ways backstory can be included in a story. *Passive backstory* might easily describe what results when the author gives us the blow-by-blow account of the protagonist working alongside his antagonist in a coal mine, and how they'd come to lose touch with each other over the past ten years because one of the pair moved out of town—until reappearing yesterday. *Active backstory* might then mean that same backstory delivered as just a telling bit, as in the Elmore Leonard example above. While the first sentence was passive, it turns active with the promise of impending action.

Active vs. passive backstory. I kind of like this as a description of the way backstory's written these days. Makes sense.

Look at the beginning sentences in Kevin Canty's short story "King of the Elephants":

> The third time we put my mother into the hospital, my father and I had already moved to Florida, to Jacksonville Beach. A cop called from D.C. at eleven o'clock one Friday night, said they'd found her sleeping on the subway, drunk, with a broken arm.

Doggie! What a great opening! The narrator tells us that this is the *third* time he and his father have had his mother committed, condensing an entire family history over many years into that one fact. We also see that the protagonist and his father have moved some distance away during that time, which implies that either they've abandoned her or she abandoned them. In a few short words, Canty has provided the skeleton of the family history, trusting the reader to supply the flesh, and he has given it to us at the proper time—at the inciting incident.

The mother has had two other breakdowns, but neither was the inciting incident. This third incident is the straw that broke the proverbial camel's back. The first two times he and his father had the mother committed were bad, in a real-life sense, but not enough to constitute a life-changing problem. The first two incidents *were* important, but only in how they set up and inform the current situation. And Canty has given them exactly as he should have—briefly and concisely, at the very beginning, to kick-start the problem of the story where it should be started.

A different (lesser) writer might have begun with some kind of weepy, I'm-a-victim sort of opening, with an overdeveloped section of unnecessary backstory and setup, such as:

> My father and I had moved to Jacksonville Beach, Florida, a couple of years ago from Washington, D.C., not so much for the better weather as to escape the emotional turmoil that my mother continually created. When I was six, she was institutionalized when she tore off her clothes and mashed bananas all over her and walked through the neighborhood braying like a donkey. Then, at my sixteenth birthday, she did it again, this time smearing Fig Newtons all over her nude body and attempting to board the E Street bus.

And so on and so on, ad infinitum, taking us blow by blow throughout the mother's entire mental health history.

Look for ways to encapsulate a lengthy history into just a few telling words. You won't slow the read for the reader by making her plow through paragraphs or pages of past events, the details of which aren't really important or necessary to the story, when only the fact that they took place is.

By the way, this is how we teach ourselves how to write—by stealing the techniques of other writers. As T.S. Eliot said, "Mediocre writers borrow; great writers steal." That doesn't mean we plagiarize work; rather, it means we take a close look at how the writer achieved an effect, and use that technique ourselves. Personally, I steal from others constantly. When I'm writing a novel, for instance, I'll have an average of perhaps thirty novels open, and I constantly look through them to see how others achieved the effect I'm looking for. Were I writing a story about a man who suffers mental and emotional abuse from his long-time boss, until something happens to finally force him to take action against the man, then I would be fortunate to come across Canty's opening here, and I would adopt the technique for my own problem. In such a story, I might write something like:

> By the fourth time that Mr. Meadows raged at him in the monthly sales meeting, Smathers had already begun to consider tentative plans to find other employment. Maybe he'd go to corporate and talk to the big enchilada himself. Or, maybe he'd just buy a gun.

In such an instance, I would have "stolen" Canty's method of delivering backstory, but without plagiarizing him in the least.

You're allowed to do the same.

BALANCING SETUP AND BACKSTORY IN YOUR OPENING

There are some stories that absolutely must begin with a lengthier setup and some backstory (the exceptions I alluded to earlier in this chapter). Usually, such tales intentionally use a fairly bucolic and placid opening to set up the *Wham!* of the inciting incident. The intrusion of the story problem into the ordinary world delivers a dramatic punch to readers, with the backstory and setup creating a sort of calm before the storm, so to speak. Fish-out-of-water stories also tend to require a lengthier setup. Stories in which early context is crucial to the reader's ultimate understanding of the story's message need longer setups as well. Finally, frame stories, stories in which prologues and epilogues are used to bookend a story, also draw on more backstory and setup to achieve success. Let's take a closer look at each of these types.

Exception 1: The Calm-Before-the-Storm Opening
This sort of opening is just what it implies. The writer shows a world at peace, and then shatters that world with the inciting incident. This kind of opening depends on

a leisurely setup to make it work. The trick is to not let the serene world go on too long—it probably should be kept to no more than a couple of paragraphs, or a page or two at most—before introducing a drastic change in that world. The danger in making this kind of beginning too long is that the reader may grow bored with what she perceives to be an entire novel plodding along in the same direction.

One of the ways to get around this is to sprinkle the narrative of that ordinary or apparently unexciting world with bits of humor. The very funny novel *A Dirty Job*, by Christopher Moore, does just that. This book is a great example of a beginning that starts out calmly and with the utmost of bucolic and mundane settings. The protagonist, Charlie Asher, is shown during his wife Rachel's labor and delivery of their new daughter, who they'll name Sophie. The novel begins like most of Moore's—with a fairly innocuous scene in which Charlie is the quintessential worrywart father, obsessing over all kinds of imaginary ailments he's sure his new baby is afflicted with (including his insistence to the nurse that his daughter has a tail). There are plenty of chuckles and outright laughs in the opening, and the reader is all set for a comedic romp. After Charlie is finally banished from the recovery room by his wife, who's had enough of his fretting, he leaves, only to return when he discovers her favorite CD lying on the seat of their car—and walks back into the hospital room to discover his wife has died.

Here's a representative bit from the calm-before-the-storm opening Moore provides. For the past half hour, Charlie's wife has been doing everything she can to get him to leave the hospital room so she can get some rest. She's at the end of her rope.

"Okay, I'll go." He reached to feel her forehead. "Do you have a fever? You look tired."

"I just gave birth, you squirrel!"

"I'm just concerned about you." He was not a squirrel. She was blaming him for Sophie's tail, that's why she'd said squirrel, and not doofus like everyone else.

"Sweetie, go. Now. So I can get some rest."

Charlie fluffed her pillows, checked her water pitcher, tucked in the blankets, kissed her forehead, kissed the baby's head, fluffed the baby, then started to rearrange the flowers that his mother had sent, moving the big stargazer lily in the front, accenting with a spray of baby's breath—"Charlie!"

"I'm going. Jeez." He checked the room, one last time, then backed toward the door.

"Can I bring you anything from home?"

"I'll be fine. The ready kit you packed covered everything, I think. In fact, I may not even need the fire extinguisher."

This is most definitely a calm-before-the-storm opening! In the hands of a lesser writer, it may have worked badly; in Moore's capable and talented mitts, it borders on genius. He lulls us into a false sense of security—we are convinced we're in for a light romp, and then—*Bam!*—we're smacked in the face with an absolute tragedy. This is a very dangerous tactic—to lead using one direction and then completely reverse. Most writers would have difficulty making this tactic work, but Moore shows how it can be done successfully. It works because he uses humor to hold our interest until he gets to the surprise shift in the character's world, and he also uses an engaging and interesting voice to help keep the reader seated and turning pages. Moore is the sort of extraordinary writer who has the talent and skill to render even a grocery list interesting to read. If you don't yet possess that kind of skill, you might want to avoid this type of opening technique until you acquire the necessary skills to bring it off.

It helps to think of this type of story beginning as the character's "world at rest." Another wonderful story that depends on a calm-before-the-storm opening for maximum effect is Raymond Carver's "A Small, Good Thing."

The story begins:

> Saturday afternoon she drove to the bakery in the shopping center. After looking through a loose-leaf binder with photographs of cakes taped onto the pages, she ordered chocolate, the child's favorite.

This opening paragraph, along with the two paragraphs that follow it, go into detail about the particulars of the birthday cake the mother orders for her eight-year-old son, Scotty. The opening paragraphs also describe the baker and his demeanor (unsmiling, businesslike, stolid). Carver gives us a clear picture of the man doing his usual business and a portrait of the mother as a fairly average mom, buying a birthday cake for her pride and joy. She comes across as a fairly sophisticated, well-to-do suburbanite, probably a liberal, politically, while the baker is listening to country music, the image of a conservative, most likely. Carver is setting it up to be a cultural and social clash on the surface, although, at the end, the reader sees that both of these people are more alike than they are different. This bit of initial conflict goes a long way in establishing a sense of foreboding.

Plus, the fact that the mother is ordering a birthday cake promises something not so good is about to happen, just because of the nature and conventions of short stories. We can assume, because the event has made it into print, that trouble is afoot. After all, it's a convention that in a story in which everything seems normal and calm, all that is about to change. Use that convention yourself. Begin a story with normality, and then deliver on what readers expect. Disrupt that world and do it pretty quickly. The reason this type of story is a convention is because stories that find themselves in print have satisfied the rules of the convention. They've begun calmly and then interrupted the calm with something bad. You'll need to do the same or you won't get your story published.

There are several ways to introduce a sense of foreboding. Using the weather is a tried-and-true method. An otherwise pastoral scene interrupted by the sudden flash of lightning and the grumbling of thunder is going to convey a rough time ahead. Another way to create a sense of foreboding is to, metaphorically speaking, throw a small stone onto the calmness of the water Carver did that in this opening by flat-out stating it with the words:

> He made her feel uncomfortable, and she didn't like that.

The woman is in an innocuous setting, but the picture Carver goes on to paint of the baker is anything but. His demeanor hints at trouble. The waters are calm and still, but yet there's the slightest riffling of the water's surface with the depiction of his manner. Paint a serene picture if you want to begin that way, but place something discordant in the corner of the picture. The reader will pick up on even the slightest mustard seed of trouble and expect it to blossom.

There are other clues. Her son's birthday is obviously a major event in the woman's life, while the baker simply sees the cake order as another job to do, further magnifying the fact that this is a story about classes clashing, as much as anything. She actually wonders why the baker doesn't appear to be as excited about her son's birthday as she is. Neither character has any empathy for the other's life, and each feels superior to the other.

Chapter Four

Carver then uses a space break—a few blank lines—to signal a shift in time as well as point of view, and then delivers the next paragraph, which includes the inciting incident. (Virtually the only times a space break should be used as a transition is when signaling an abrupt departure from the present scene, followed by either a different point of view, a switch in geographic location, or a shift in time, forward or back.) The setup in Carver's story is brief—those first three paragraphs—and most setups that are necessary to make the story work should be fairly brief. Ground us in the character's world at rest before the onset of the story problem, but deliver this setup as succinctly as possible. And include at least the hint of trouble to come. The inciting incident occurs after we are thoroughly immersed in the story's "world at rest," when Scotty is struck by a car on his way to school.

The inciting incident becomes infinitely more dramatic because we've seen his mother in the bakery buying his birthday cake. We've gotten to know his family a little bit—seen that his mom is a regular kind of soccer mom and all that—and so we care a lot more about him than we would have if Carver had just deposited us into the story with him getting hit by the car. We know she's a mother who loves and cares about her little boy, and that causes us to care deeply when we see him get struck by the car.

We also sense that, even though the boy appears to be okay, there's going to be more to the accident, and so there is. The boy will eventually end up slipping into a coma and dying, and the mother will of course have forgotten all about the cake. The baker will begin calling their home, irritated at first that she hasn't come in to pick up her cake (which has not been paid for), and gradually becoming more and more incensed at what he perceives as her theft of his time and work. In the end, there's a confrontation, and two people make a connection and gain a new understanding of their little corner of the human condition. If you haven't read this or any of Carver's stories, do yourself a favor and do so. He's a wise, intelligent writer—my personal favorite. Not to mention that he's a master not only at writing stories, but at beginning them in a good place.

When constructing a good calm-before the-storm opening, avoid creating a *boredom*-before-the-storm opening instead. Even though you're creating a snapshot of a normal world that's about to be shattered or significantly changed, you shouldn't write a boring account of that world. One way to maintain interest is to make the setup humorous, as Christopher Moore did in *A Dirty Job*. Another technique is to show conflict or at least a contrast between characters, as Raymond Carver did in his story. And always use a scene to deliver that world. Don't open with the narrator's passive thoughts describing that world. Always remember that anything important in a story should be expressed through a scene and not through exposition or summary. The opening is one of the most important parts in any story.

Exception 2:
The Fish-Out-of-Water Opening

Lengthier setups and backstory are also necessary in fish-out-of-water stories, which depend on an early and memorable contrast between the narrator/protagonist and the situation in which he finds himself. George Singleton's "Outlaw Head & Tail" provides an example of this approach:

> Normally, I couldn't have made the tape that Saturday. Right there during the job interview a few weeks before, Frank, my soon-to-be boss, had said, "Rickey, is there anything about this job that you have a problem with?"
>
> I didn't say, "I can't work for a man who ends sentences with prepositions." I couldn't. It was a job bouncing, or at least talking. I was going to be something called a pre-bouncer. If some guy came into the Treehouse and looked like he meant trouble, I was supposed to go up to him and start a little conversation, let him know this wasn't the kind of place to throw a punch without inelegant and indubitable consequences.
>
> I had a way with words. I'm synonymous with rapport.

We need to see the contrast between the narrator and the world he's in for the fish-out-of-water story to work, and this brief setup/backstory accomplishes that. Singleton also establishes the "rules" of reading this particular story, showing us an unreliable narrator: He has this job as a kind of bouncer, but obviously isn't the bouncer type; he's a verbal man, not a physical one. And we get a pretty good idea that no good is going to come of this situation. Which is the case.

Notice that there's an instant push against the stereotype here. We usually associate a certain type with barroom bouncers, and the protagonist definitely doesn't fit the image we have.

The author lets us know in the very first sentence that there's going to be a problem—something is not normal. The first sentence also contains a bit of essential backstory and setup, informing us of something that took place before the inciting incident; it's necessary we know there was a tape made. Of course, we don't know what tape the character is talking about, or even what kind of tape it is, but we are delivered a story question right from the start. What's this tape, and why is it important? Many great stories include the whole of the story in the first paragraph, and so does this one. The tape the character refers to is a tape of his wife's delivery of their baby, and he ends up taping an episode of the TV show *Bonanza* over it. This act stands for everything wrong in his marriage (and himself), which is what the story is all about.

Exception 3: The Essential-Context Opening

A third instance in which a longer setup is crucial is when a deeper sense of context is needed to establish mood and set the stage for the events to come, as in Sherman

Alexie's novel *Indian Killer*. Alexie begins this story with a long, detailed setup of a hospital. In the case of this novel, such a lengthy setup was perfect, since the novel's principal theme (message, even) is a cultural one—Native Americans vs. white America, as exemplified by the saga of protagonist John Smith's life—and that made it necessary to give the reader context to make sense of the events that follow the setup. A longer setup and backstory is essential here, because the whole thrust of the novel depends on the contrast we see at the beginning. If Alexie had omitted this lengthy beginning and depiction of the Indian world, if he had excluded this truly relevant historical backdrop, it would have been difficult if not impossible for the reader to grasp the full implication of what happens to John Smith. The story begins:

> The sheets are dirty. An Indian Health Service hospital in the late sixties. On this reservation or that reservation. Any reservation, a particular reservation. Antiseptic, cinnamon, and danker odors. Anonymous cries up and down the hallways. Linoleum floors swabbed with gray water. Mops smelling like old sex.

The opening goes on in a similar vein, painting for the reader a myriad of rich details about the hospital and the characters that populate it, all leading up to an Indian woman's childbirth taking place. It's actually the protagonist's childbirth, and he's imagining how it took place, rather than describing it as a witness.

There are several things about this particular opening that are instructive.

First, it begins with a hint of trouble. "The sheets are dirty." If that doesn't signal a character's universe out of kilter, nothing does. In a sense, this first sentence encompasses the whole of the novel. The sheets are representative of how Alexie views the Indian condition—they are literally born into a "dirty" world. We learn in the very next sentence that this is a hospital, a place where we expect a sterile environment and, certainly, clean sheets. We also are given definitive clues that this is an imagined description when we see descriptions such as, "On this reservation or that reservation. Any reservation, a particular reservation."

Alexie skillfully segues from this detailed description and setup into the backstory of his character, beginning with the moment John Smith was born, even though the narrator is not reporting on that incident as a witness, but imagining how it went. Notice, too, that the backstory information is being included in the present of the scene, and the story continues chronologically until the end. As we discussed earlier, backstory usually interrupts a scene in the form of a flashback or a memory of something in the past by the narrator, but that's not the case here. Instead, this story begins with John Smith imagining his birth and then imagining his adopted parents and how they came to their decision to adopt him, and it continues until his death.

John's imagining of his birth is the inciting incident, because it is through this imagining that he's awakened to his story problem—he's a misfit in a white-dominated world. This is a novel designed to personalize the Native American condition in this country. It's as much an anthropological treatise as it is a novel. In a case like this, it's appropriate that the character's very birth is the inciting incident, since it's that event that launched his story problem—surviving as a Native American in an alien white world. The circumstances of that birth are important in illuminating not only the problems faced by most Native Americans, but, particularly, his character's own problem. The birth John is imagining becomes more fantastic as he imagines himself being torn from his teenage mother's arms by a nurse, rushed to a helicopter landing outside, and handed over to a man in a white jumpsuit. All unlikely events, but what John is imagining to be the truth of his birth.

From the birth he imagines as an adult, the story segues into what he imagines happened prior to that birth; this is the backstory. The narrator goes from his birth, to the white couple that adopted him at birth, and to what led them to adopt an Indian baby, and then into the rest of the story.

Keep in mind that these kinds of examples are the exceptions, not the rule in story beginnings. Most of the time, your story should begin in one place only, and that's with the inciting incident.

Exception 4: Frame-Story Openings

For those who don't know what a frame story is, it's simply where the bulk of the story is enclosed within a couple of bookends, "framing" it. This structure is ideal for stories in which a prologue is needed to balance out a first chapter that opens with a lengthy chunk of backstory. In such cases, the prologues can be used to provide readers with a hint of the inciting incident that's to come, thus ensuring they'll sit through the crucial backstory that must (note the use of must here) be provided up front. Framing also helps in stories in which the narrator is looking back on the story, perhaps in the form of an adult recalling a childhood experience.

Larry Watson's novel *Montana 1948* is another example of a story that succeeds at least partly because of this structure. After a brief prologue in which the skeleton of the inciting incident is briefly given, the first ten pages of chapter one are mostly concerned with introducing the reader to the harsh, unforgiving landscape of mid-nineteenth century Montana, as well as the unique history and place narrator/protagonist David's family occupies in the town, information vital to understanding the events that follow.

While I don't know this for a fact, I suspect Watson's story structure—especially his beginning and ending, represented by a prologue and an epilogue—were perhaps agent- or editor-inspired and may not have been included in the manuscript he submitted originally for consideration. This is pure conjecture on my part, but my own publishing experience suggests to me that this may well have been the case. I suspect the prologue and epilogue were included to create a frame story to serve as a marketing tool. I did the same with my novel *The Death of Tarpons* upon the advice of literary agent Mary Evans. Just like *Montana 1948*, my own novel is centered on a summer in the life of a young (fourteen-year-old) boy. *Tarpons* was rejected countless times (well, okay—it was rejected exactly eighty-six times ...) and may have remained to this day "only available in my room," had I not had an encounter with Evans when my manuscript was used in a workshop she conducted in Indianapolis many years ago. She praised the novel, but said it was "virtually unpublishable" because of the sex and age of its protagonist, Corey John. First, she told me, they (agents and publishers) will see it as a young adult novel and not as an adult novel.

I was flabbergasted. Since I saw it as an adult novel, I was trying to market it that way and hadn't presented it as a YA at all. The concept that agents and editors were seeing it as a YA had never occurred to me. Sure, my character was a young kid, but so was the protagonist in John Knowles's *A Separate Peace,* and no one saw that as a YA. Evans said it didn't matter and pointed out that the single worst book-buying demographic in the U.S. is young boys. It turns out most guys at that age don't read. At least not as much as other identifiable groups. Therefore, publishers are loathe to publish a novel centered around the life of a member of that particular group. She told me that one of her own clients, Pulitzer Prize-winning novelist Michael Chabon, had experienced the same sales resistance with his own first novel, *The Mysteries of Pittsburgh*. She recommended I do what she'd had Chabon do and that was to create a frame story. In my case (and in Watson's as well, whether by agent or editor influence or not), the bookends consisted of beginning the narrative with the protagonist as an adult and then going directly into the story of the child, and then re-emerging to the adult looking back again at the conclusion.

That strategy, Evans said, would make it appear to be an "adult" book and get a more favorable read and possible publication.

Well ... it did. It got that favorable read and publication, because I did what Evans suggested. (I never got to thank you, Mary Evans, so I hope you read this and know how grateful I am.) The very next publisher I sent it to after reforming it into a frame story (University of North Texas Press) sent me a contract.

I'm including my own little story here for two reasons. First, to give a plausible reason why *Montana 1948* is constructed in the manner it is with the prologue and epilogue featuring the narrator as an older man looking back. And, secondly, I'm hoping that perhaps there's an author or two out there who has been desperately trying to peddle his own manuscript that is structured in the same way as my original manuscript for *Tarpons* was who will find frame story structure useful. If that happens, let me know! It'll make my day.

Anyway, the beginning of Watson's book is in the form of a short prologue written by the adult narrator David Hayden looking back at the summer of his twelfth year in a brief, one-paragraph setup, and then plunging directly into the story, delivering a sketch of the inciting incident, and then going into a lengthy backstory before picking up again with the inciting incident as presented briefly in the prologue.

Montana 1948 begins:

> From the summer of my twelfth year I carry a series of images more vivid and lasting than any others of my boyhood and indelible beyond all attempts the years make to erase or fade them. ...

My own novel begins:

> Not long ago, I returned to the town of my youth, and made a disturbing discovery. It had weathered the intervening thirty years better than I had, at least physically, and that had the effect of giving me a bit of a jolt, as if the events of the last summer I spent there, the summer of my fourteenth year, hadn't been as cataclysmic as I'd imagined.

Both of our first paragraphs are all telling, summarizations, and neither includes a scene or an inciting incident.

They're setup, pure and simple, to let readers know who's speaking here and what his stance in the novel will be.

The lines immediately following the opening paragraph in Watson's novel break into italics and into the story itself, and give glimpses of what we will eventually see to be the beginning of the inciting incident.

> A young Sioux woman lies on a bed in our house. She is feverish, delirious, and coughing so hard I am afraid she will die.
>
> My father kneels on the kitchen floor, begging my mother to help him. It's a summer night and the room is brightly lit. Insects cluster around the light fixtures, and the pleading quality in my father's voice reminds me of those insects—high-pitched, insistent, frantic. It is a sound I have never heard coming from him.
>
> My mother stands in our kitchen on a hot, windy day. The windows are open, and Mother's lace curtains blow into the room. Mother holds my father's Ithaca twelve-gauge shotgun, and since she is a small, slender woman, she has trouble finding the balance point of its heavy length. Nevertheless, she has watched my father and other men often enough to know where the shells go, and she loads them until the gun will hold no more. Loading the gun is the difficult part. Once the shells are in, any fool can figure out how to fire it. Which she intends to do.

What makes Watson's prologue work is that he not only delivers the skeleton of the inciting incident, he places the protagonist's parents in moments of great tension and emotional distress. This allows the somewhat mundane (but necessary) backstory to be delivered, as the reader has been vividly shown that some dire moments are forthcoming. Even though all he delivers here is a glimpse of the inciting incident and resultant surface problem, it's enough of a snapshot to let the reader know a momentous shift has occurred in the protagonist's life and that we're going to get to it, by and by.

Was his prologue necessary? Not really. The story could have begun with the full scene of the Indian housekeeper, Marie, coming down with her fever and what emanated from that triggering incident. The history delivered after the prologue and before the full inciting incident scene of Marie could also have been delivered after taking the reader through Marie's fever and the surface problem that occasioned.

Immediately following the brief prologue, chapter one goes into backstory with a slow, measured description of the area and its history and of the place the narrator's family occupies in it. It gives the history not only of the narrator's father (who will be the protagonist) and how he came to inherit the office of sheriff from his own father, and also of the history of his brother, who will be his antagonist. It's a version of the Cain and Abel story and, as such, requires this history be absorbed by the reader before the story proper begins.

Perhaps sensing that the reader is beginning to get fidgety after reading for these first pages about a family and a region, Watson even includes this sentence near the end of his history lesson:

> This was our family in 1948 and those were the tensions that set the air humming in our household. I need to sketch in only one more character and the story can begin.

It's as if Watson senses that even though it's necessary in this particular story to begin slowly, he's about to lose his reader if he doesn't provide a promise that all this is about over and he's gonna get to the good stuff soon.

The next (and last) character during this prehistory that he introduces is Marie, the live-in Indian house-keeper the boy's family employs. It's Marie's illness and her subsequent murder that provide the trouble in the story. We already know from the prologue that she's going to be at the center of the trouble of the story. Once the backstory is conveyed and Marie's illness is discovered, the story picks up a new tension and pace and the struggle is on.

But, without those ten pages of family history preceding it, the affect of her death on the family wouldn't have had nearly the same emotional impact as without it. This is one of those stories in which delivering backstory early works for a variety of reasons. One is because we've already seen, albeit briefly and via the prologue, the inciting incident and the powerful reactions of the father and mother and from that know that we'll return to that drama. Two, the power of the language itself serves to keep the reader's interest during this passive period. And three, even though it's history, it's presented in an engaging and interesting way. It's not just related dryly, but is also liberally sprinkled with tension and chock-full of trouble and the promise of trouble. The land is harsh and unforgiving, as is the patriarch of the family. The father is somewhat crippled, and he and his brother are painted as adversaries. The father and mother have an ongoing rift as she wants to move to a more "civilized" place and have him give up his job as sheriff and become a lawyer, which he won't do.

By and large, I wouldn't advise going so quickly into backstory for most books, but if your material is similar to Watson's, it works if done skillfully.

I have to relate something else about this truly wonderful book. I picked it up one night at the recommendation of a friend, intending to read a few pages and then drift off to slumberland. Four hours later, I hadn't put it down and was as wide-awake as if I'd just learned that the Unabomber had just moved to our neighborhood.

And when I finally reached the end of the novel, and there was an "Afterword" by David Huddle, the judge for the Milkweed National Fiction Prize, that read:

> The morning I picked up the manuscript of Larry Watson's *Montana 1948*, I meant merely to begin it, to read at most

> thirty or forty pages. By the end of the afternoon I had
> completed its last page and my mind was full of it.

The exact same experience I'd had! Later, I turned to the reviews of it and many of the reviewers had had the very same experience with it. They'd picked it up, intending to read a few pages ... and couldn't put it down until they finished it.

This is the kind of book I trust you want to also write. I know I do. Read its beginning and see how Watson pulls off this literary feat with the opening. You'll be glad you did.

A Final Word of Caution

Should you opt for a lengthy setup to your opening scene: Some writers—in particular, *young* writers—have a great desire to be thought of as different or original. To achieve this reputation, some adopt the tactic of breaking as many rules as they can. Do this at your own peril—you may gain the reputation of being original or eccentric, but most of the time that description will also earn another adjective: *unpublished.*

Breaking rules doesn't make one original—pick out any juvenile delinquent loitering on a street corner and you'll see what I mean. Working within the rules and delivering original and creative stories is what makes one original.

And successful.

CHAPTER FIVE

Combining the Inciting Incident, Story-Worthy Problem, Initial Surface Problem, Setup, and Backstory

Now that we've seen how each of the primary components (and backstory!) functions on its own, let's take a closer look at how they function *together* in an opening scene. First, a quick review of these elements.

The opening scene features the inciting incident, which is the dramatic event that creates the initial surface problem and sets up the introduction of the story-worthy problem, which is the raison d'être for the entire story.

Backstory is all that has gone on before the inciting incident.

And the setup is just that—whatever it takes to let the reader understand what's going on when the inciting incident occurs. The setup can also include a bit of backstory, but most of the time backstory isn't necessary. Usually, the setup is brief. Perhaps all that's needed is to show a man and a woman sitting in a restaurant and the man speaks.

FITTING THE PIECES TOGETHER

Let's look at a few books and movies for examples of how all the elements of a good opening work together to produce a memorable story and how that opening organically segues into the rest of the story. Then, we'll take a more in-depth look at how the components function within Christopher Moore's *Island of the Sequined Love Nun*.

As you read through the following examples, keep in mind that you might find it helpful to create similar outlines for films and stories you come across. This will help you grasp how all the elements fit seamlessly together when you write your own novel. That said, when you look at these outlines remember that you'll likely encounter stories, novels, and movies that don't contain all of the elements I'm claiming here contribute to good openings. The reason for this is that all stories—in whatever form—are flawed. There is no such thing as a "perfect" opening. No one yet has written the perfect novel or film or short story. Stories succeed in spite of their flaws. The purpose here is simply to help you write as close to a good opening as possible and give yourself the best chance at being read and ultimately published. The closer you can come to creating openings that work, the better your chances of getting that novel you're laboring over published.

I've said words to this effect before in these pages, but it bears repeating. It will be very easy to pick up a popular movie at your local video store or the current bestseller at your local bookstore, and, after viewing or reading it, show conclusively how that particular story didn't follow all or even many of the precepts advanced here. If you look again at the film or the book, you will probably discover an element that was so powerful that it overcame the weakness of a poor beginning. That happens. The question is, do you want to depend on that kind of thing carrying your own work? It makes more sense to have both that powerful component of your work going for it ... plus a great opening, doesn't it?

Now, on to the examples. Let's look first at a movie:

> **Title**: *A History of Violence*
>
> **Opening Backstory**: None
>
> **Setup**: We get a sense of how dangerous the bad guys are, and we see the protagonist, Tom, as a loving husband and father (i.e., in his "world at rest").
>
> **Inciting Incident**: The bad guys threaten Tom's customers and attempt to rob his diner. (Remember: An inciting incident is something that happens to the protagonist, creates the initial surface problem, and introduces the story-worthy problem.)
>
> **Initial Surface Problem**: To remain passive or take action to protect himself and his customers from the bad guys.
>
> **Initial Surface Goal**: To protect those around him and, therefore, must take action.

Story-Worthy Problem: To find a way to reconcile his violent past from which he can no longer hide.

Story-Worthy Goal: To gain acceptance and forgiveness for his violent past from his family.

Once the inciting incident has taken place, the course of the story is set. Tom's attempt to resolve his initial surface problem (killing the bad guys to protect his customers) ends, as do all his attempts to resolve his problems (until the final act, of course), in disaster. The disaster? While it appears he is successful—after all, he's saved himself and his customers from harm—this act lands him on the television news where mobsters from his former life see him and show up in town with the goal of forcing him to return to his brother (who now runs the mob) to answer for the crimes he committed in his "old" life. This creates a string of interconnected surface problems that slowly work to expose the true nature of Tom's story-worthy problem.

It's a chain reaction from the very first moment, with all of the subsequent acts stemming from that first scene (the inciting incident) in which he decides to revert to his old self and kill the bad guys. Each act he takes to resolve his surface problems ends in failure while simultaneously serving to further illuminate Tom's story-worthy problem—to both himself and viewers—to resolve his past and reconcile his misdeeds with his present life and goals (his family). When the bad guys show up to bring him back to his brother, he tries to convince them they have the wrong guy. That fails and Tom is forced to defend himself and his family against their wrath. Then, in the confrontation with the mobsters, Tom is forced for reveal his violent history to his family. All of this is leads up to the final scene, in which his mobster brother calls him home to answer for his crimes against his other "family." When he gets there and his brother attempts to have him killed, Tom realizes he only has one choice if he is to gain his story-worthy goal. He has to kill his brother. That act provides the resolution he's been seeking, for both his surface and story-worthy problems. With his history of violence exposed and the blood of his brother washed from his hands (literally and symbolically as he washes his bloodied hands in his brother's lake), Tom returns home to his family in the hope of finding acceptance and forgiveness.

The second work I'll outline is Louis Sachar's brilliant young adult novel, *Holes*. I have to tell a story about this book. When my son, Mike, was about nine, he kept after me and after me to read this book. I kept promising him I would, but then I wouldn't. It was categorized as a young adult book, and I just didn't read many YAs. Finally, just to get him off my back, I decided to read it.

Boy, am I glad I did!

Holes turned out to be one of the best books I'd ever read. Once I got into it, it ceased being a young adult book and just became ... a darned good book. I recommend it to everyone of every age. Now, let's break down the opening.

Title: *Holes*

Opening Backstory: Very little is included. The curse on Stanley's family is described and a portrait painted of the young boy as an overweight kid who is unable to stand up for himself against bullying teachers and classmates. He's been convicted of a theft he didn't commit and is put on the bus to the juvie camp. (In this case, a bit of backstory is necessary, but Sachar makes it work because he does three things: he weaves it in with the "present" of the story; he makes it brief; and, he makes it interesting.)

Setup: There's a brief description of Camp Green Lake, a camp for juvenile offenders, and of the warden who runs it. There's also a quick introduction of Stanley, who's been sentenced to the camp for stealing a pair of shoes.

Inciting Incident: Stanley is sent to Camp Green Lake and his world is irreversibly changed.

Surface Problem: To find a way to survive Camp Green Lake and the warden's wrath.

Surface Goal: To return to his family.

Story-Worthy Problem: To overcome his imagined inheritance of a family curse, which has formed him into a person who expects to be a victim.

Story-Worthy Goal: To become a self-sufficient young adult who no longer allows himself to be a victim.

Try creating a short outline like the examples given here for a few stories or films as you read or watch them and you'll quickly come to gain a thorough understanding of how all the pieces fit together in an effective opening. After you've done a few, you'll come to the place where you can almost instantly see if the author's opening is strong or weak, and, more importantly, you'll develop the tools to write your own powerful openings.

DECONSTRUCTING A BRILLIANT BEGINNING

Now that we've looked at a few general outlines illustrating how the pieces of an opening fit together, let's go a little deeper and take a more comprehensive look at an opening from a wonderful author who really knows how to begin a story properly. All of Christopher Moore's wacky, laugh-out-loud books are bestsellers, largely because he knows how to begin his stories in the right place. That he writes exceedingly well also helps, as does his irreverent and humorous take on his material, but if he didn't give the reader great openings, chances are his wonderfully droll stories would not have even gotten read, at least by his first reader (his editor or agent). I suspect there are a great many writers who write as well or nearly as well as Chris does, but who have never had their work exposed to the public, simply because they began badly.

Anyway, let's take a look at the beginning of Christopher Moore's *Island of the Sequined Love Nun*, which opens with the inciting incident:

> Tucker Case awoke to find himself hanging from a breadfruit tree by a coconut fiber rope. He was suspended facedown about six feet above the sand in some sort of harness, his hands and feet tied together in front of him. He lifted his head and strained to look around. He could see a white sand beach fringed with coconut palms, a coconut husk fire, a palm front hut, a path of white coral gravel that led into a jungle. Completing the panorama was the grinning brown face of an ancient native.
>
> The native reached up with a clawlike hand and pinched Tucker's cheek.
>
> Tucker screamed.
>
> "Yum," the native said.
>
> "Who are you?" Tucker asked. "Where am I? Where's the navigator?"
>
> The native just grinned. His eyes were yellow, his hair a wild tangle of curl and bird feathers, and his teeth were black and had been filed to points. He looked like a potbellied skeleton upholstered in distressed leather. Puckered pink scars decorated his skin; a series of small scars on his chest described the shape of a shark. His only clothing was a loincloth woven from some sort of plant fiber. Tucked in the waist cord was a vicious-looking bush knife. The native patted Tucker's cheek with an

ashy callused palm, then turned and walked away, leaving him hanging.

"Wait!" Tucker shouted. "Let me down. I have money. I can pay you."

The native ambled down the path without looking back. Tucker struggled against the harness, but only managed to put himself into a slow spin. As he turned, he caught sight of the navigator, hanging unconscious a few feet away.

"Hey, you alive?"

The navigator didn't stir, but Tucker could see that he was breathing. "Hey, Kimi, wake up!" Still no reaction.

He strained against the rope around his wrists, but the bonds only seemed to tighten. After a few minutes, he gave up, exhausted. He rested and looked around for something to give this bizarre scene some meaning. Why had the native hung them in a tree?

He caught movement in his peripheral vision and turned to see a large brown crab struggling at the end of a string tied to a nearby branch. There was his answer: they were hung in the tree, like the crab, to keep them fresh until they were ready to be eaten.

Tucker shuddered, imagining the native's black teeth closing on his skin. He tried to focus on a way to escape before the native returned, but his mind kept diving into a sea of regrets and second guesses, looking for the exact place where the world had turned on him and put him in the cannibal tree.

The inciting incident (the plane crash) lands Tucker in a tree where he's immediately faced with his initial surface problem (the threat of being eaten by a cannibal) and sets the stage for his story-worthy problem (his life-long immaturity). After the opening paragraphs, Moore segues wonderfully into the backstory/setup material. The reader scarcely knows it's happening, it's so seamless. There's no clumsy "He remembered how it all happened, a year before ..." kind of stuff going on here. We're in the hands of a master.

> Like most of the big missteps he had taken in life, it had started in a bar.
>
> The Seattle Airport Holiday Inn lounge was all hunter green, brass rails, and oak veneer. Remove the bar and it looked like Macy's men's department. It was one in the morning and the bartender, a stout, middle-aged Hispanic woman, was polishing glasses and waiting for her last three customers to leave so she could go home. At the end of the bar a young woman in a short skirt and too much makeup sat alone. Tucker Case sat next to a businessman several stools down.
>
> "Lemmings," the businessman said.

And so begins the backstory. Seamlessly. Moore doesn't even find it necessary to signal this with a space break. We're firmly hooked into the story and not about to put it down and take a break, because we left Tucker hanging in a tree, about to become a cannibal's lunch. This opening is a great example of a technique called entering late and leaving early. We enter the story late, in the sense that we don't know how Tucker got tied upside down from a tree. We leave the opening scene very early, since it obviously isn't over. Most readers will be more than willing to sit through some backstory now—the protagonist and his problem are extremely interesting. Also, Moore's writing style assures us that even though he's going back in time now for some setup and backstory, whatever we read there is going to be captivating as well. He has proved in a short page and a half that he knows how to write captivating prose and knows how to tell a story.

Let's see, the protagonist, Tucker; a Hispanic bartender; a babe in a short skirt; and a businessman are in an airport bar at one in the A.M. I'd expect something interesting to come of this cast of characters, wouldn't you? (And it does.)

Now, some of you may wonder if the backstory in Moore's novel, which begins with us being transported several months back in time to that bar, isn't really the inciting incident. Well, yes and no. One might argue that it is, because what happened in that bar led to Tucker's being captured by the native. But it isn't, because although what happened in the bar put Tucker in a bad situation, and being in that situation led to him finding himself upside down in a tree, what happened in the bar merely represents a situation. A situation that does, indeed, lead to a pretty big problem (being eaten by cannibals), but still just a situation. What happened in the bar does not reveal the story-worthy or initial surface problem. Conceivably, you could go back as far as the birth of a character for an inciting incident. After all, if your protagonist hadn't been born, there wouldn't be a story, right? A cause-and-effect chain of events could be traced, technically, back to the very beginning of time, using that kind of logic! If Adam and Eve hadn't .... or, if the primeval slime hadn't produced one-celled animals, leading eventually to humans ... (pick your own beginning according to your beliefs), then ...

For those of you who haven't read Moore's book, I will give a brief account of the backstory that begins at the bar.

Tucker's a bit of a playboy and he romances the girl in the bar in Seattle. He talks her into joining the mile-high club. (I trust no one needs an explanation of what that is.) He's the corporate jet pilot of a company that strangely resembles a famous home cosmetics sales company. The company jet he pilots is pink, which should give you a fairly good clue as to which company Tucker's resembles.

While Tucker is boinking his newest mile-high club pledge, the plane, on autopilot, hits some turbulence and he suffers a terrible accident. His scrotum is ripped down the middle and he ends up in the hospital with a lot of embarrassing press clippings to peruse during his healing period. The owner of the cosmetics company is furious over the terrible PR her company is receiving. Not only does she fire Tucker, she hints that she may send a hit man to visit him in return for all the damage he's caused her and her reputation. Plus, the FAA has lifted his license.

Enter Tucker's mentor, the guy who taught him to fly and got him in the business, who relays a job offer from a company in Micronesia to fly their company plane. As he's unemployable in the States without a license, and this is the only offer on the table or likely to be forthcoming, Tucker accepts it. It's on his trip to the island where he's to work that he ends up in the tree with the native licking his chops.

That brings us up to speed; and sure, it all really began when Tucker invited the girl to fly the friendly skies with him, but even though the plane incident landed him in a bad place and eventually led to his hanging upside down in a tree, it was still only a bad *situation*. He wasn't at the end of his rope—literally—at that point. While he couldn't get a job flying a corporate jet, he could have obtained a job doing something else. And, while the company owner and founder may have threatened him with a hit man, the threat wasn't definite, and most likely wouldn't have come to anything.

Therefore, the incident at the bar or in the plane doesn't qualify as an inciting incident. It is important backstory, however, as it shows the reader how and why Tucker ended up on the island; it needed to be included in the story. And, just about everything—from that Seattle bar to the point where Tucker finds himself in that tree—not only informs the reader as to how and why

Tucker got there, it provides dozens of foreshadowing elements that make sense of what he does later.

What's important for our purposes here is that the necessary backstory is included in exactly the right place: *after* the real inciting incident. If Moore had begun the novel with the bar scene and the subsequent unfortunate event aboard the plane, we would have felt mildly sorry for him lying in the hospital bed with a penis swathed in bandages, but that problem would not have been story-worthy. Tucker still had many options available to him. But he doesn't have much wiggle room helplessly trussed up on an island, with a native licking his chops!

It's important to know also that, while Moore's inciting incident works and works well, it's the initial surface problem that the inciting incident creates. It's a pretty good problem—being trussed upside down in a tree and on the menu for a cannibal is fairly drastic stuff and does, indeed, pose the most serious problem in Tucker's life at the time of the story. However, his story-worthy problem, as the reader will discover, is his immaturity and his juvenile approach to life. It's the way he takes on life that's his true problem, and his various surface problems will eventually reveal that to him and readers. During the course of the story, Tucker will come to realize that, not only did his immaturity lead him to being upside down in a tree, but that same immaturity led him to most of the crises in his life. When he learns that truth about himself, he achieves an insight that matures him and provides a resolution to his story problem.

Chapter Five

The one thing, though, that truly makes the island predicament the inciting incident is that it is the first time in his life that Tucker really begins to grasp that he has a serious problem. Although we don't know it yet, this is virtually the first time in his life (and his is a life that's had more than its share of bad things) that he's become aware that being in a bad place might actually have something to do with something in *him*. Some flaw in him. Before, when he found himself in a bad predicament or situation, he dismissed it as bad luck or karma or whatever; this is the first time he's begun to look inside and become aware that his own character might be the source of his troubles in life. Thus, this incident has started to expose his true story-worthy problem to him, and that's what a proper inciting incident has to do.

Like the characters in your own stories, Tucker has a backstory and a history that's important to the book. That's fine and needs to be included. It just shouldn't come at the *beginning* of the story. It should, with few exceptions, make its appearance only after the inciting incident, and be delivered to the reader as a scene that ends with both the protagonist and the reader at least somewhat aware of the story problem. Get the reader involved immediately with a scene that reveals the inciting incident and resultant story problem—and make it a worthwhile problem—and then deliver the backstory.

You'll end up with a story people will *read*. Which means a story people will *buy*. Our noble goal.

PUTTING IT ALL TOGETHER
IN YOUR OWN WORK

In preparation for writing your own beginning, the first thing you need to do is figure out what your protagonist's story-worthy problem is going to be. If you don't have that doped out yet, you really don't have a story. Let's assume you have one, though.

Perhaps you want to write a story about a guy who's part Native American, part Cuban, and part Caucasian, and his problem stems from the fact that he exists in the predominantly white world of the 1920s, in which minorities are looked down upon and treated as second-class citizens. He feels a decided lack of respect not only from his fellow townspeople, but, more importantly, for himself as well, because of his racial heritage. It's a situation he's familiar with, having lived in it all his life.

What you need to do is to write an inciting incident that will create a compelling initial surface problem and start to reveal your protagonist's story-worthy problem. Let's say you've decided to put him into a situation in which his race is involved. You might then come up with a scene in which he's fifteen years old and has just walked into the general store in the small, western town in which he lives. The owner is in the back working on filling drug prescriptions and he recognizes your boy—let's call him Carlos—and asks young Carlos what he wants. Just an ice cream cone, Carlos says, and the owner tells him to help himself and just put the money on the counter. So Carlos makes himself a peach ice cream cone and is putting the nickel on the counter when two men wearing suits come in. Carlos recognizes them—they're both notorious bank robbers. The owner sees them from his little window, and tells Carlos to go ahead and help them, not recognizing them as Carlos has.

The two outlaws had originally planned just to buy some cigarettes and some Unguentine—they were bank robbers, not stickup guys—but when they see the situation, they see the way to some easy bucks. They begin by messing with Carlos, taking his ice cream cone from him. They ask him his name and one of the outlaws says he doesn't look Mexican, and Carlos says he's not, he's part Cuban. The outlaw laughs and says Cuban's the same as Mex. He tosses the boy's ice cream cone on the floor. They then order your guy Carlos to open the cash register and give them the money. They haven't pulled out their guns, but they've let Carlos see them in their belts. The owner still doesn't know anything's wrong.

Just then, you have another man—a Native American by the name of Junior Harjo—enter the store while Carlos is taking the money out of the cash register for the outlaws. On the surface, it still doesn't look like a robbery to anyone except Carlos. The owner looks up from his little window and sees the guy who's just entered, recognizes him, and calls out that he's got his mother's medicine ready. Then he says to Junior that his mother mentioned he'd been raiding Indian stills, looking for moonshine, and asks Junior to hold a jar aside for him. This alerts the two outlaws that there's a lawman in the place, and they proceed to shoot and kill Junior Harjo and run out and get in their car and drive away.

What this scene reveals to Carlos is that he's not considered a real man because of his Hispanic blood. He's been aware most of his life that folks treated him with less respect than they would a white man (a little bit of backstory and setup), but this incident brings it home to him in a way that simple insults and insulting behavior never have. His very manhood has been challenged. From that point on, he makes it his mission in life to find and capture these outlaws. Doing that, he feels, will give him his manhood and the respect that goes with it.

In creating a scene like this, you've given Carlos both his surface problem—capturing the outlaws—and his story-worthy problem—the lack of respect from the white world. His goal—to capture the outlaws—will earn him that respect.

See how that works? Now, I'd say you could use this inciting incident for your own, but you'd probably better clear it with Elmore Leonard first, because this is how his novel *The Hot Kid* begins. The important thing is to see how you can use the same strategy in coming up with your own beginning. Just ask yourself, "What can I do to create a scene that will introduce my character's *real* problem?" Get that right and the rest of the story becomes a lot easier!

CHAPTER SIX

Introducing Your Characters

Thus far, we've looked individually at the inciting incident, the story-worth problem, the initial surface problem, the setup, and backstory, and we've taken a look at how to put together an opening that incorporates those elements. In this chapter, we're going to look at another important element that should permeate your opening: character. Elements of character should always be present in your opening and there are several ways to accomplish that.

ESTABLISHING CHARACTER FROM THE START

Toni Weisskopf, the publisher of Baen Books, believes that one of the biggest bugaboos in submitted manuscripts is when the author doesn't clearly identify the protagonist. She wants to know quickly the protagonist's sex, age, and level of sophistication in the world the protagonist operates in. She needs to know this and other details about the protagonist because the readers won't be much interested in that character until they know about her and who she really is. Readers will feel fairly chilly toward a character who begins with an emotional response to something the readers haven't also witnessed. Readers' interest in the protagonist has to be earned, in other words.

That doesn't mean you should give long, detailed descriptions of characters at the beginning of your story. A complex picture can be painted in very few words by a skilled writer. There are many ways to do this. Physical description is only one, and is usually the weakest method. Dialogue is another. Describing a character's station in a particular society is another. There are literally dozens (if not hundreds) of ways to create a portrait in just a paragraph or two.

Here's an example from one of my own short stories, "My Idea of a Nice Thing":

> She woke up at three in the morning, like she'd been doing for more than a week now, and her brain was buzzing, all kinds of thoughts flying around in there, so she used the trick she'd come up with, of lying perfectly still and picturing a single goldfish swimming in a small fishbowl. The next thing she was conscious of was the alarm ringing in her ear and her mouth being dry and her head hurting. And she wanted a drink in the worst way.

After a space break, the second paragraph reads:

> "So I drink," she said, the first time she stood up at A.A.
> "My job. I'm a hairdresser. See, you take on all of these
> other people's personalities and troubles and things, ten
> or twelve of 'em a day, and when the end of the day
> comes, you don't know who you are any more. It takes
> three drinks just to sort yourself out again, bring the real
> you up to the surface." That brought scattered laughter.
> Someone started a basket around for contributions.

There's lots of information about the character (Raye)
here. She's just "hit her bottom" in alcoholic parlance
(which is the inciting incident that reveals the story
problem, her alcoholism) and her first action to combat her addiction follows swiftly after, when she decides
to go to Alcoholics Anonymous. We see she's a woman
of some imagination by the stratagem she's employed to
forestall her drinking urges and seek sleep (visualizing
the goldfish) and it may be interesting that she hasn't
chosen some clichéd trick such as counting sheep; her
technique shows the more imaginative turn of her
mind. A person under the stranglehold of addiction is
a person many readers will feel sympathy and empathy
for—and perhaps even identify with—and you should
always strive to create protagonists that elicit at least two
of those elements from the reader, especially sympathy
and empathy. Identification is more of a hit-or-miss
proposition, and you can't always create characters that

all of your readers can identify with, but the other two are attainable, provided you create and describe your characters with care and skill.

We learn Raye's occupation (hairdresser), as well, which is an excellent way to paint a character's picture. In this country and most others, what one does for a living informs how one is viewed and even how we view ourselves. It's what we "are." We're engineers, housewives or househusbands, factory workers, dentists, second grade teachers, whatever. Writers.

We also learn what kind of hairdresser Raye is. She's one who views her job as somewhat more than just a job. She gets into her clients' lives ("you take on all of these other people's personalities and troubles") and the way she interacts with her customers also affects her mental state and is at least a contributing factor in her alcoholism ("and when the end of the day comes, you don't know who you are any more. It takes three drinks just to sort yourself out again, bring the real you up to the surface."). We see that although Raye may not alibi her addiction away completely, she at least does the human thing of excusing it somewhat by how attentive she is to her clients. Thus, she's a bit of an unreliable narrator, but not much more so than the average person who is in a bit of denial. It's excusable, in other words, and most likely endears her a bit to the reader. Another human quality.

And then, the A.A. audience responds with "scattered laughter." At least some of the people gathered there show that they're behind Raye and on her side, and as social creatures, when we as readers see others responding positively to a person in a tale, we tend to do the same toward that same person. It's much the same effect as when we hear a joke in a comedy club and the audience responds with hearty guffaws—we usually do the same. We laugh a bit harder and louder simply because others do, and we instinctively know it's acceptable to do so. We're all susceptible to peer pressure, and it's no different in fiction. Have other characters in your stories like your protagonist or respond to her favorably, and you tip the scales in favor of readers liking her as well.

And, if we like a character, then we want to see her do well and we're willing to follow her around and invest our time and interest in rooting her on in her struggle. But, as Toni Weisskopf advises us, it's important we know something about the character so we can get to like her.

The trick is to avoid standalone description or exposition of your character's personality and appearance, and to instead show the reader your character by putting her in action. A character's physical description—unless markedly different than the norm—does relatively little to draw the reader in. The character's actions are much more useful. Or details such as their occupations and interests. The readers will furnish a perfectly good description on their own if you simply let them know that the Uncle Charley of your story is a butterfly collector, or the elderly toll-gate keeper on the Suwannee River.

Doing so will accomplish more than ten pages of physical description, listing hair and eye color, height, weight and all of that kind of mundane detail. In fact, my own writing contains very little description of any of my characters—it's virtually nonexistent—yet, for years I've asked readers if they can describe a character I pick at random from my stories, and invariably they come up with a detailed description, no matter which character I might choose. When I tell them I haven't described the character mentioned at all (as I hardly ever have), they're surprised, and some swear that I did, even going so far as to drag out the story and look for where I've included the description. They never find it.

The point is, physical descriptions of characters is way overrated and the poorest way to give the reader a mental picture of your character. Physical description is only valuable if it actually means something in the story: For instance, a character with a pronounced limp—a limp that is crucial to his character—runs the Boston Marathon and wins.

Best-selling British writer Nick Hornby starts his novel *How to Be Good* by taking us through his protagonist's inciting incident revealed in an action that is contrary to her normal behavior and personality.

> I am in a car park in Leeds when I tell my husband I don't want to be married to him anymore. David isn't even in the car park with me. He's at home, looking after the kids, and I have only called him to remind him that he should

write a note for Molly's class teacher. The other bit just sort of ... slips out. This is a mistake, obviously. Even though I am, apparently, and to my immense surprise, the kind of person who tells her husband that she doesn't want to be married to him anymore, I really didn't think I was the kind of person to say so in a car park, on a mobile phone. That particular self-assessment will now have to be revised, clearly. I can describe myself as the kind of person who doesn't forget names, for example, because I have remembered names thousands of times and forgotten them only once or twice. But for the majority of people, marriage-ending conversations happen only once, if at all. If you choose to conduct yours on a mobile phone, in a Leeds car park, then you cannot really claim that it is unrepresentative, in the same way that Lee Harvey Oswald couldn't really claim that shooting presidents wasn't like him at all. Sometimes we have to be judged by our one-offs.

Wow! Don't you wish you'd written that? I sure do!

While we are being taken through her story-problem-creating crisis, we learn a great deal about protagonist Katie Carr. First, she comes across as surprised and amazed at her own behavior, which she herself views as diametrically opposed to the kind of person she is. She's just not the type (at least in her own mind) to blurt out her desire for a divorce to her husband over a phone. The implication behind the words is that she's fairly dumbfounded that she'd even consider a divorce, much less announce she wants one not in person—face-to-face—but over the phone. The readers suspect that they've perhaps come across an unreliable narrator, and unreliable narrators almost always carry the promise of at least some fun (for the readers) in a story. It's just plain fun to try to figure out the truth of a character from the clues the author provides.

Or, it may be that this really is her true character and that it took a cataclysmic event (her marriage break-down) to force it to the surface. In either event, this opening promises an intriguing read and it does so by what's shown of the character in action. She's saying she's a woman of no surprises—that she lives her life in a conventional and probably even boring fashion—but then she performs a totally unconventional (for her) action. Who wouldn't want to read on to find out why she's acted in this way? Quite a few couldn't resist—this novel ended up a *New York Times* bestseller.

A third, very different example of establishing the protagonist's character from the very start is found in crime novelist Michael Connelly's *Lost Light*.

> There is no end of things in the heart.
>
> Someone once told me that. She said it came from a poem she believed in. She understood it to mean that if you took something to heart, really brought it inside those red velvet folds, then it would always be there for you. No matter what happened, it would be there waiting. She said

this could mean a person, a place, a dream. A mission. Anything sacred. She told me that it is all connected in those
secret folds. Always. It is all part of the same and will always be there, carrying the same beat as your heart.

I am fifty-two years old and I believe it. At night when
I try to sleep but can't, that is when I know it. It is when all
the pathways seem to connect and I see the people I have
loved and hated and helped and hurt. I see the hands
that reach for me. I hear the beat and see and understand
what I must do. I know my mission and I know there is no
turning away or turning back. And it is in those moment
that I know there is no end of things in the heart.

What makes this opening different? Well, it's by a brand-
name author with a sizeable audience already in place. Michael Connelly's books have made the best-seller lists at
least nine more times than I've hit a grand-slam walk-off
home run at Yankee Stadium as a member of the Bronx
Bombers. What does that mean? It means that he can
write just about any opening he wants and it's going to get
published. It means that in the hands of a writer without
a ready-made audience such as Connelly enjoys, opening
with the protagonist's bit of philosophy might not work. It
could easily come across as sentimental or self-indulgent.

There is, however, another factor at work here. Connelly writes detective novels and his protagonist here, Hi-
eronymus Bosch, is a character he uses a lot. Nine times,
in fact, at the time of this book. Nine bestsellers. One reason a series character becomes popular is because of some

bit of individuality that endears the character to the readers and makes him interesting. One of Bosch's quirks is that he is a deeply philosophical man. He's not just a guy who runs around solving crimes. He only picks crimes to solve that he has a philosophical interest in, usually an aspect of something he (Bosch) perceives as a character flaw in himself. Solving the crime is a way for Bosch to work out his own psychological problems. Which is the reason that Connelly's novels transcend genre and can be honestly considered literary as well as popular. They are as much about the inner psychological life of a character as they are about the crime to be solved.

From this beginning and from Connelly's previous novels, we know that the protagonist is going to take us through a quest that will expose the innermost workings of his secret self, a place he's loath to go because of what it might reveal about himself. That is always what the best literature does—it exposes the author's darkest places through the character on the page. We know that everything that happens from now on in the novel will be related to this opening, that we are going to see a man struggling to fulfill his mission, which is to be the person who speaks for the victims.

Does that mean that you can't create such an opening if you aren't a famous author? Not at all. It just means that you have to be careful and make sure that you deliver what you promise with such an opening. Throughout the rest of the story, the reader needs to see clearly that your protagonist is going through whatever he's going through because of the philosophy stated in the opening. Do that, and you may end up with a series character as well.

You should also make such an opening short. Connelly's opening here is about three-quarters of a manuscript page in length. Much more than that and his opening could easily have degenerated into something melodramatic or even maudlin. He goes directly from a brief bit of philosophy (208 words, to be exact) into the story itself.

We also see that this is a detective with a deep soul and a thoughtful, reflective mien (and this may be the most important thing). What the author chooses to reveal about his character is telling. This is a character worth knowing better—a character with depth.

We also see from the beginning that there's trouble ahead. The narrator has already told us he's about to be engaged in a dark struggle, a struggle as much against himself as against his on-stage murderer-as-adversary.

And so we read on. As will your readers, should you craft such a beguiling opening.

OPENING WITH
UNUSUAL CHARACTERS

Beginning with an out-of-the-ordinary character or cast of characters can instantly pique the reader's interest. It goes without saying that there must be more to such an opening than weird or quirky people—it still has to have trouble develop immediately—but such an opening can be an effective preamble to the story problem that follows. Let's look at a Barry Hannah short story, "Fans," for such a beginning:

> Wright's father, a sportswriter and a hack and a shill for the university team, was sitting next to Milton, who was actually blind but nevertheless a rabid fan, and Loomis Orange, the dwarf who was one of the team's managers.

Hold up your hand if you wouldn't want to read about this merry band. Okay—I see you, way in the back. Feel like you're in a club of one? A dwarf, a blind man, and a sell-out sportswriter? Nothing but weirdness can possibly come from this group.

The trouble begins quickly after this introduction, when this motley crew gathers in a bar. As readers, we're with them because we want to see what happens to such an odd mix of characters.

Another example of opening with an unusual character is the one Sherwood Kiraly wrote in his rollicking novel *Diminished Capacity.*

> My uncle Roland Zerbs lives in LaPorte, Missouri, where I grew up. He's known locally as the Fish Man.

I want to know more about somebody the locals have dubbed the Fish Man, don't you? The promise of that opening is fulfilled very quickly, when we learn that Uncle Roland's obsession in life is to publish a volume of poetry written by the fish that live in the Mississippi River, which rolls by his house. To get the fish to accomplish this literary task, Uncle R. has placed an old Royal typewriter on his pier and has affixed a hooked and baited line to each of the keys, each dangling down into the water at differing lengths. Uncle Roland then cleans up (edits) the output of the fish (who are mostly perch), taking what appears to be liberties with his editing efforts.

We can imagine what his neighbors think of him, and it's probably not all positive.

Some fun. Some opening. How can a writer not write a super book when he begins like this? How can a reader resist reading it? If your story is about a wacky guy doing wacky things, it needs to begin with him doing something weird.

Another situation that works well is to show a "normal" character doing strange things, as in fish-out-of-water openings. Those openings place a character outside her normal milieu. An example would be taking a teenage girl born and bred in lower Manhattan and plunking her down on a dairy farm in Wisconsin.

OPENING WITH YOUR CHARACTER'S THOUGHTS

Opening with your character's thoughts can be very effective, but you have to be careful that you don't begin with a character ruminating about some past dreadful event—or even the inciting incident *after* it's occurred.

I've found that to be one of the biggest mistakes student writers make—getting inside a character's mind (actually, their own minds) and delivering the story via the character's thoughts, rather than allowing the reader to experience the story dramatically at the same time the character does.

This is where the advice "show, don't tell" may be confusing. Most of the time, we take that advice to mean that we should create a scene in which characters are interacting. But sometimes a scene is actually a view of what's happening, entirely from the perspective of the character, without other characters interacting with her. Such a scene is possible (and sometimes necessary) when the inciting incident is an event witnessed in solitude by the protagonist, or is experienced by the protagonist while surrounded by others who have nothing to do with the event. If it's that event that creates and reveals the story problem to the character, and there's no one else interacting with her at the time, it's still a bona fide scene. In the case we're going to look at in a minute, that's exactly what happens, and it works just fine.

At a story's beginning, we need a scene that we can live through with the protagonist as his initial surface problem is created. We can't do that with the sequel to a scene, in which the protagonist is merely (and dully) reflecting on that event. Let us be as surprised as the protagonist is, and we'll have nearly the same emotional reaction as she does. And when that happens, you've hooked the reader!

A wonderful example is the beginning of James Baldwin's short story "Sonny's Blues." It begins:

> I read about it in the paper, in the subway, on my way to work. I read it, and I couldn't believe it, and I read it again.

He goes on to describe his shock at reading some article in the paper. Even though we are witnessing the experience from the narrator's thoughts as he lives through it, this is not passive prose at all, and not what I meant when I admonished against writing a character ruminating in her head. This is instead a fully realized and delivered dramatic scene. It's not the author "telling" us what's happened; it's the narrator/protagonist delivering the scene as it happens so that we're there to experience what he does at the same time he experiences it. This event can't be delivered in the normal mode of dramatic scenes, i.e., via character's interactions, simply because it happened to the protagonist when he was, for all purposes, by himself. He's reading of his brother in the newspaper, and that act of reading is profoundly changing his world at the instant his brain processes what he's reading. Exactly what an inciting incident does. We don't know yet that it's his brother he's reading about, but we will shortly. What we do know is that he's reading this article and it creates a great shock in him. We get his response to the article at exactly the same time he does.

Therefore, we believe it and are instantly drawn into the story. Why? Even though we don't know yet what it is he's read, from his reaction we know something serious has just rocked his world.

And we want to know what it was that had that effect. So we read on. The purpose of a good opening, right?

The second paragraph keeps the scene going, making it more complete and showing clearly how this news article has changed the protagonist's world. This paragraph shows us the character's emotional response to the article, and "big-dealizes" it. We experience the character's emotion at the same time he does, and that's powerful. It gets us firmly on his side. The scene is presented so there's no doubt in the reader's mind that this is the biggest single problem in the protagonist's life at the time. He can function—barely—but nothing supercedes the problem that's been thrust upon him.

> It was not to be believed and I kept telling myself that, as I walked from the subway station to the high school. And at the same time I couldn't doubt it. I was scared, scared for Sonny.

The rest of the paragraph goes on, in great descriptive detail, about how the article has affected him emotionally.

The third paragraph reveals what Sonny has done—been busted for selling heroin. We still don't know quite who Sonny is or what his relationship with the narrator is, but this only creates more tension. We also get strong evidence that the narrator and Sonny have a long history. We may even suspect they are related. What we do know is that Sonny has been arrested in a big enough bust that it's made the newspapers, and that's significant in a large town (most likely, from clues like "in the subway," New York City), where most crime goes unreported or is reduced to small agate, if mentioned at all. This is also where the first backstory is introduced. *After* the inciting incident.

The fourth paragraph reveals what Sonny's relationship to the narrator is.

> ... I didn't want to believe that I'd ever see my brother going down, coming to nothing, all that light in his face gone out, in the condition I'd already seen so many others.

We now know that Sonny is his brother. After all the buildup, Baldwin pays off. This is truly an epochal change in his life. Baldwin "big-dealizes" the inciting incident. If it's a big deal to the narrator/protagonist— and we see that it truly is—then it becomes a big deal to us, the readers, as well.

The scene begins with a very few paragraphs that contain far more information and emotion than a mere mortal's paragraphs ought to be able to! It then goes from this, the opening scene containing the inciting incident, into how the protagonist deals with it, and then includes some backstory. Baldwin published this in 1957, but it could have been published yesterday and met the requirements today's stories have to meet to draw the reader into the story. In more than one way, Baldwin was far ahead of the herd.

It's particularly important to note that even though Baldwin gets us inside his protagonist's mind, he isn't delivering that kind of rumination I've warned against. He doesn't write, for instance:

> I remember reading about it in the paper, in the sub-way, on my way to work. I read it and I was horri-fied. I couldn't believe it and I read it again. My God, I thought.

And so on. Delivering the scene that way takes it down to the level of a character merely cogitating. Baldwin is simply using the perspective of the character's mind to deliver what he's experiencing, not dwelling on his take on it, so that it becomes simply a reverie.

You can use his example for your own work. Let's say you want to write a story about a woman who's just learned she's been adopted and isn't the natural child of her parents, as she always assumed she was. You can have her find this out by coming across an old diary written by her mother when she cleans out the attic after her parents have been killed in a car accident, and you can employ the same technique Baldwin did.

It's neat how this stealing stuff works, isn't it!

CHAPTER SEVEN

Foreshadowing, Language, and Setting

Foreshadowing, language, and setting. These are not insignificant opening elements. While the inciting incident, story-worthy problem, initial surface problem, setup, and backstory dominated so much of our earlier discussion, the components we're going to explore in this chapter are themselves worthy of careful dissection. To varying degrees, depending on the story you're writing, each plays an important role in rounding out a believable opening.

USING YOUR OPENING TO FORESHADOW YOUR STORY

Openings that foreshadow events to come either work well or fall as flat as the earth was before Christopher Columbus gave it a new shape along with his new route to India. The latter (the route to India) has been proved to be somewhat incorrect, but the earth's shape thing is still considered okay by most of us. Not all openings provide a foreshadowing of the end or of an impending important development, but a disproportionate number of the best do. That said, it isn't the end of the world if your story doesn't. Remember what I said about many stories succeeding in spite of obvious flaws and because they contain another element that's powerful and overcomes the weakness? But I do strongly suggest that you consider including at least a hint of what's to come in your opening. Take a look at the following examples, and I think you'll agree that foreshadowing can strengthen and even "make" a good opening.

Foreshadowing strives to let the reader know that the issues to come are larger than the reader might assume. Foreshadowing may even tell you explicitly that something big is about to happen. The author who chooses this kind of opening wants the reader to clearly understand what's at stake.

An excellent example of such an opening is the beginning of best-selling thriller writer Jeffery Deaver's novel *The Coffin Dancer*:

> When Edward Carney said good-bye to his wife, Percey, he never thought it would be the last time he'd see her.

Rather than let us live through this scene to begin with and draw our own conclusions, Deaver lets us know that a seemingly innocuous event is going to turn out to be much more important than it might first appear.

Another fine example of an opening that foreshadows the story is in William Goyen's short story "Tongues of Men and of Angels":

> I started out to tell about what became of two cousins and their uncle who loved them, according to what the older cousin told me. But some of their kinfolks' lives would have to be told if you're going to talk at all about the cousins and their uncle. So what I have to tell about first is all one family, what I heard told to me and what I watched happen. I have been here in this family's town longer than any of the family, and have in my long time noted—and wonder if you have, ever—the turning around of some people's lives, as if some force moved in them against their will: runaways suddenly arrived back, to the place they fled; berserk possessed people come serene; apparently Godblessed people overnight fall under malediction.

This most certainly provides the message to the reader to stay tuned! It also says that big trouble lies ahead. The story is a family saga, but the point of view is narrowed down to one character—the narrator/protagonist—and the story problem is his, created by the family dynamic.

Another such opening is found in Ellen Gilchrist's "Some Blue Hills at Sundown," her short story about a six-teen-year-old girl trying to seduce a dying college student who will end up refusing to deflower her.

> It was the last time Rhoda would ever see Bob Rosen in her life. Perhaps she knew that the whole time she was driving to meet him, the long drive through the November fields, down the long narrow state of Kentucky, driv-

ing due west, then across the Ohio River and up into the flat-topped hills of Southern Illinois.

We don't know why Rhoda won't ever see Bob Rosen again in her life, but most of us will certainly want to stick around and find out why! Something momentous is obviously going to happen. We also want to know who Rhoda is and who Bob is and why she is going to see him. We'll just have to read on to find out. This opening fits perfectly the advice William Zinsser offers on proper beginnings in his book *On Writing Well*. He says, "The most important sentence in any article is the first one. If it doesn't induce the reader to proceed to the second sentence your article is dead. And if the second sentence doesn't induce him to continue to the third sentence, it's equally dead. Of such a progression of sentences, each tugging the reader forward until he is hooked, a writer constructs that fateful unit, the 'lead.'"

Zinsser is talking here about nonfiction articles, but the same principle holds just as true for fiction, if not more so. It holds true for any piece of writing that the writer wants the reader to keep reading. Certain nonfiction articles may find readers simply because of their content—an engineer, for instance, may need to read a treatise on the support properties of cement, and will therefore plow agonizingly through pages of boring prose out of necessity. Fiction readers don't have that kind of gun to their head, except perhaps in literature classes. Fiction has to be even more well-written simply because of the nature of the audience—which happens to be a *volunteer* audience, not conscripts who are forced to read by the demands of a profession or job or even a hobby, and for whom the content is more important than the writing itself.

In fiction, we gotta give 'em a reason beyond content to read on.

ECONOMIZING LANGUAGE IN YOUR OPENINGS

Economy of language doesn't mean using fewer words. It simply means that every word needs to count and to represent much more than the few syllables it takes to utter. A grand example of an opening story sentence that practices such economy is found in Jamaica Kincaid's "Xuela":

> My mother died at the moment I was born, and so for my whole life there was nothing standing between me and eternity; at my back was always a bleak, black wind.

An entire lifetime expressed in a very few words! Signaling, of course, a story about what else?—*trouble.* The protagonist's inciting incident is when her mother dies and leaves her with her father, who passes her off to the unloving woman who washes his clothes. The opening goes on to illustrate graphically how the protagonist survives a bleak and sterile childhood. Kincaid encapsulates the entire backstory and inciting incident into one sentence. Pretty good writing, eh?

Here's another example, the opening two sentences of Raymond Carver's short story "Gazebo":

> That morning she pours Teacher's over my belly and licks it off. That afternoon she tries to jump out the window.

Damn! An opening pair of sentences doesn't get much better than this! The whole of the story is right here. The protagonist's wife goes from the heights of joy and ecstasy to the despair of attempted suicide in the space of a few hours. It's a story about how protagonist Duane's infidelity affects his wife, Holly, and their subsequent inability to find their way back together; and it is my personal favorite of all of Carver's stories (of which I'm a huge fan). An obvious great example of economy of language, Carver's opening satisfies other requirements of good openings, one being that a good opening should contain at least the seeds of the ending.

Eschew the flowery language you may think makes you look literary, and just tell a story clearly and interestingly. An agent or editor encountering a bunch of ten-dollar words three paragraphs into the read, isn't going to give two cents about the rest of the story. You do the math on that. Don't have a character regurgitate his evening repast when all he really did was blow chunks of his hot dog.

Some editors have a particular bias against particular words. My bias is against the word *plethora*. I still think it's the ugliest, most pretentious word in the English language. And, for some reason—probably because of sins in a past life—I seem to get a plethora of student stories containing the word every semester.

Another thing that raises the hackles ever so slightly is when writers spell the word *okay* as *ok* or *O.K.* Just feels like e-mail language. Or, when they do things like abbreviate *Iowa* to *IA*, or *suite* to *ste*. Just feels *lazy*. We're talking about two lousy keystrokes. Every editor has a personal list of words that irritate, and you can't possibly know which words affect each person, but if you just keep the ten-dollar words out of the prose when a two-dollar one or a fifty-center does good work, you'll be all right.

Using Specificity and Details to Help Create Strong Openings

As we just saw in the examples above, it's possible to use specific details to paint vivid pictures in a few words. Let's look at another example and see how a well-placed word or three can really make opening sentences sizzle. Look at how Dennis McFarland begins his short story "Nothing to Ask For"—with specific details to raise story questions and emphasize the state his protagonist is in:

> Inside Mack's apartment, a concentrator—a medical machine that looks like an elaborate stereo speaker on casters—sits behind an orange swivel desk, making its rhythmic, percussive noise like ocean waves, taking in normal filthy air, humidifying it, and filtering out everything but oxygen, which it sends through clear plastic tubing to Mack's mouth.

Who is Mack and why is he hooked up to this machine? Has he been in an accident or does he have some lung disease like emphysema? Or has his lung perhaps been punctured by a switchblade in a street fight? These and other questions are instantly raised in this beginning, and we naturally have to read on to find out the answers. We see by the specificity of language that this machine is important. Specific details like this in good stories are never there just as scenery, but stand for something important— something to pay attention to. And so it is, as we see later in the story. Mack is the protagonist's lifetime friend and gay lover and is dying of complications from AIDS. They both reminisce about their years together, and while each sees the events of their lives together differently, just as the machine takes in "normal filthy air" and humidifies and filters out "everything but oxygen," so does the narrator/protagonist, filtering everything his friend relates to get to the pure oxygen of the meaning of their relationship. A marvelous opening, in which the specificity of detail plays an important role.

One more. From Barry Hannah's short story "Getting Ready":

> He was forty-eight, a fisherman, and he had never caught a significant fish.

Wow. One word enables this sentence to transcend the mundane to the sublime. Can you guess what it is? The adjective *significant*. Without that one specific word, this sentence would probably be a lie—it's fairly certain that anyone who calls himself a fisherman has caught at least *one* fish. If any other adjective had been used, the impact of what the narrator is relating would have been lost or at least diminished. Substitute the word *big* for *significant*, for instance. Ho-hum. See what I mean? This sentence implies, because of the protagonist's age and the way in which the sentence is delivered, that the narrator has been a fisherman all of his life—which makes it even sadder that he has never caught anything of importance. Those who perceive themselves as anglers are often measured by the tales they can tell of the giants they caught, as much as by the stories of the ones that got away. Up until the moment of this story, the protagonist has never achieved anything, and, knowing the nature of stories, we can assume his failure to land anything momentous in his fishing life is a metaphor for his very existence, and so it is. Not only hasn't he ever caught a significant fish—he's never achieved anything significant in his entire existence. Until the time of this story, that is.

Sentences built with strong verbs and concrete nouns go a long way toward enriching openings. Don't settle for the first general verb or first fuzzy noun that comes to mind. Pare down and rework your sentences until they come alive with energy and meaning, and, most of all, until they deliver a complete image to the reader. Show, don't tell.

Another technique for maximizing the impact of a sentence is to reserve the action of the sentence for the end. The end of the sentence is what the reader remembers, and placing the action at the end rather than at the beginning gives a sentence its biggest impact. Compare "He had never caught a significant fish, even though he was forty-eight and had been a fisherman all his life" to what Hannah actually wrote.

Do the same with your sentences and you'll begin to create powerful scenes and images for your reader.

Beware of Clichés, Adverbs, and Adjectives

You're a writer—use original language. Watch out for clichés. Clichés are born when someone, somewhere, comes up with a truly original bit of language, probably to describe something. It is so original that other writers and speakers glom onto it. It gets overused. It becomes a cliché. Be the kind of writer who comes up with such inventive phrases that others will eventually transform into clichés. One of the joys of reading is to be surprised and delighted with new turns of phrase. An agent or editor who encounters one of those will be delighted, and your work will gain valuable coin with her.

Remember, too, that good writing is created from strong verbs and concrete nouns. When an editor sees adverbs sprinkled liberally in a text, she knows she's got a poor writer on her hands. Or at least a lazy one. Almost as bad is the overuse of adjectives.

And keep in mind that you can still err when you do use strong verbs and concrete nouns if you keep using those same distinctive verbs and nouns over and over again.

INTRODUCING SETTING IN YOUR OPENINGS

It is by all means okay to open with place or setting, provided, as always, that the setting is crucial to the inciting incident and story problem. Some writers make their settings a character in the story, as William Faulkner did with his mythical Yoknapatawpha County, and as Raymond Chandler did with Los Angeles. Ellen Gilchrist is another author who often uses setting to jump-start her stories and novels as well as to inform them. In "The Tree Fort," Gilchrist deals with a young girl's first awareness of how she is destined to fit into a male-dominated world when she becomes an adult, and she begins with both a town and a specific and concrete artifact of that town—a fort constructed of Christmas trees.

> I have been haunted lately by memories of Seymour, Indiana. A story in a magazine set me off and set me dreaming, of my brother, Dudley, and the fort, and the year he lost the eye. A fort made out of Christmas trees, piled four trees high, on the flat ground where the yard ran down to meet the alley. Dudley's pyramid, a memorial to the light in his left eye.

Gilchrist evokes a place, and not just a place, but a *particular* place—a Midwestern kind of place in which kids build forts out of Christmas trees. Discarded Christmas trees—especially in the numbers described ("piled four trees high")—aren't objects readily available in, say, Jerusalem or Morocco, nor are they likely handy for such purposes in Queens, New York, in at least the sections where Orthodox Jews live; this is an archaeological kind of thing that is peculiar to a relatively limited number of places and times. In these politically correct times, for instance, kids building military forts aren't as common as they were even a few years ago. This is a town that has an *attitude*, much as individual people have attitudes.

When you treat the place or setting as an important character, it makes perfect sense to allow that place to open the story, just as any other character would. The trick is to weave that setting seamlessly into the inciting incident scene itself, rather than to provide a kind of windowpane (passive) description that stands alone. And don't simply include poetic prose in the description indiscriminately. Instead of describing the mountains of West Virginia with such terms as "purplish hills" and "kudzu-covered mountainsides," use descriptions such as "flinty shale lying just beneath topsoil too thin to sustain any kind of decent crop" to inform the protagonist's life as being hardscrabble. Any description should illuminate the character in particular ways.

CHAPTER EIGHT

Great Opening Lines

Your first sentence or paragraph may be the most important writing in your story. They may well be what sells your manuscript to an agent or editor. Look at people browsing in a bookstore or library. Watch how many open the book to the first page and read for twenty seconds or so. They're reading those first sentences to see if this is the book that will capture their Visa or MasterCard charge. If the first sentence doesn't grab them, there's little reason to go on and, more importantly, to plunk down their plastic.

Here's a tip. Editors and agents do the same thing when they cover the manuscript you've sent them. Some of those folks don't read much further than the opening sentence or two. A great first line buys you an awful lot of points. An agent or editor coming upon a terrific opening sentence or paragraph is infinitely more inclined to read more of the story than he would be if the opening is ordinary. Unoriginal opening sentences usually lead to unoriginal stories.

Your first sentence is your door into the house of your manuscript. Do you want that door to be inviting, attractive, intriguing? Or do you want a door that whimpers, "The Mundanes reside here. Enter at the risk of falling asleep"?

No-brainer.

A great opening sentence can swing that door wide open. Of course, the rest of the story has to live up to the promise of the opening lines. The thing is, if you start your story properly, the rest comes much easier. Keep in mind that the beginning is a part of the whole. An opening created properly will contain at least a hint of the end when the reader looks back. In fact, as author Cynthia Ozick advises, "If you're writing a story and are confused about the end, go back to the beginning." Very often, you'll find the solution to the problem of creating a good ending in that sentence. Recently, I had a student approach me about the ending of the story she was working on for class. I passed Ozick's advice on to her, and an hour later, back at my office, I was delighted to open an e-mail from her—excitement jumping off the screen—that said she'd gone back to her beginning, and the solution to how to end the story had magically come to her. Those are great moments for a teacher. Pointing someone toward the place a student can find an answer for himself is immeasurably more satisfying than merely giving the answer.

What should be in an opening line? Anything that provokes the reader into reading the second one. And the third, and the fourth—you get the picture. Provided that the line opens the story where the story should open—when the trouble begins—many elements can be present in an opening line or paragraph. Mystery, intrigue, shock, a revealing glimpse of an interesting and original character that promises excitement or some other strong emotion to come—whatever. Your opening lines should incorporate many of the opening scene elements we've discussed, such as characterization, setting, powerful language, and the setup. The important thing is that what you open with presents a question that the reader will want to answer. The one thing that shouldn't be present in opening lines is exposition.

Let's look at some examples of opening lines that grab the reader and pull him with a firm yank into the story. After reading the sentences below, the first thing you need to do is ask yourself "Would I read further?" I'm confident the answer will be a resounding and assertive yes. The second thing you need to do is write lines like these writers did!

───────────────── ⟗ ─────────────────

From Luisa Valenzuela's short-short "Vision Out of the Corner of One Eye":

> It's true, he put his hand on my ass and I was about to scream bloody murder when the bus passed by a church and he crossed himself.

We see a scene in which a man has taken an obviously crude, if not criminal, action; and then, immediately, we see he has another side to him that we didn't expect. We know we're in the company of a couple of pretty unusual, interesting, and complex characters, and that something we haven't seen before is about to happen. Actually, it's in the middle of happening. An arresting image like Valenzuela has provided here is guaranteed to spark reader interest.

This is an author who's learned to enter scenes late and leave early, and that's one of the keys to writing good scenes. As we've discussed, writers feel a temptation, especially when writing the opening scene, to preface the action with backstory and setup. In many cases, this is a big mistake. Simply make certain the reader knows what's going on, who the people are, and what their relationships are, and do this with the context of the scene itself and not with summary or exposition.

———————————— ❧ ————————————

From Robert Hill Long's short story "The Restraints":

> Even when she was very little her hunger was worth something: hunger taught her to dance, and her father noticed.

Wow. Who wouldn't want to read further to learn more about such a character and to find out what her relationship with her father was? Her hunger wasn't important to him; her dancing was. I'd like to know about a character like this. Wouldn't you? This is obviously going to be a relationship story, and if you can deliver original ways to show the state of the relationship, like Long did here, your story is going to get read.

From K.C. Frederick's story "Teddy's Canary":

> And Louise calls him down—she's screaming her head off because the pipe just blew totally and water's shooting out from under the sink and Bernie must think she's popped an artery or something and he's out of that bathtub like a goosed whale.

I don't know about you, but I'd absolutely have to read on to find out what's happening in this explosive opening, and how it turns out. Not to mention that the language is specific and funny, and this sounds like a good fun ride to climb onto. Give the reader a strong, particular voice like this and you gain his undivided attention.

From Sherman Alexie's short story, "What You Pawn I Will Redeem."

> Noon.
>
> One day you have a home and the next you don't, but I'm not going to tell you my particular reasons for being homeless, because it's my secret story, and Indians have to work hard to keep secrets from hungry white folks.

Okay. I cheated on this one. I gave you *two* opening sentences. But the first sentence, "Noon," is short enough

Hooked

that I hope you forgive me. Does anybody doubt that even though the narrator has said he's not going to reveal his secret story, he's lying, or that if we read on we'll find out what the secret is? What reader can resist reading on to find out? Alexie's also given us a clear protagonist and antagonist, and we see a war that's a continuation of the war Native Americans have been fighting since the Vikings first landed on their shores. This is an example of a tease opening, and comes from an unreliable narrator, perhaps the best kind of narrator for comedy and irony. An unreliable narrator is one who says one thing when his actions say another. A great example is the third-grade teacher on the first day of school, being asked by a fellow teacher in the lounge what she thinks of her new class. She replies, "Oh, I just love every single one of my kids! Even that little Jenny White with the funny clothes and the dirty face." We hear her saying she loves all her kids, but do we believe her? Of course not! She's already shown us that she thinks less of little Jenny. (Remember that dialogue is considered action in fiction.) You can use an unreliable narrator for intelligent humor or even for powerful drama, as Stanley Elkin does in his classic "A Poetics for Bullies" or as Eudora Welty does in her short story "Why I Live at the P.O."

―――――――――――――――――〇―――――――――――――――

From Ron Carlson's short story "Milk":

> They almost fingerprint the children before I can stop them.

What children? What's happened? Sure looks like a crime has been committed and a serious one at that—they don't fingerprint folks unless a capital crime has been committed, except on TV. Cops don't dust for fingerprints for a mere burglary, for example, unless the amount stolen is huge. And why on earth would children be fingerprinted? Get this story and read it to find out. I had to. Create a mystery in your opening and the reader is yours.

From Douglas Glover's novel *The South Will Rise at Noon*:

> Looking back, I should have realized something was up as soon as I opened the bedroom door and found my wife asleep on top of the sheets with a strange man curled up like a foetus beside her.

Glover not only sets the tone here (ironic humor—this isn't the usual response of a man who finds his wife sleeping with another man), he raises all kinds of questions with this opening. Questions no reader can resist reading on to find the answers to. This narrator is a masterful understatementalist. (How 'bout that? I just made up a word!) Bottom line is, if you give the reader an unexpected response to an event, as Glover does here, you've got that reader in the palm of your hand.

From my own short story "The Bad Part of Town."

> He was so mean that wherever he was standing became
> the bad part of town.

Many times, fledgling writers want to know how established authors come up with ideas for stories. (With a bit more experience, they'll come to realize that ideas are never a problem—that ideas are everywhere and most of us will run out of time in our lives before we can use even one-hundredth of the ideas that come our way. But, at the beginnings of their writing careers, many don't yet know this.) Ideas come from everywhere. The impetus for this story came one evening when I was standing talking with a group of friends just before a reading was to take place at Vermont College, where I was in residency for my MFA in writing. There were perhaps seventy to eighty people in a large room, and all of a sudden a man I didn't know appeared at the far side of the room.

Because I spent time incarcerated, and because I lived for a large portion of my life among that part of the populace termed "criminal," my eyes were instantly drawn to this guy. When you live and interact with criminals—and are, in fact, a criminal yourself—you develop a kind of antenna that alerts your self-preservation instinct to potential danger. In other words, when a truly bad guy makes an appearance, you know such a person is present. Whether it's by the way he carries himself (probably), or a look in his eyes, or whatever, you just *know* that here's a person not to be messed with. A *dangerous* person. He doesn't signal this in the Hollywood way—by dress or by some bit of acting learned via Stanislavski—but in just the tilt of his head or the cant of his eyes. You just know.

And, even though this guy was clear across the room and I suffer from nearsightedness, I knew instantly that this was a guy you didn't mess with. I asked somebody who he was and discovered that the story about him was that he'd been an enforcer for a South American drug cartel for many years. It had been this guy's job to do whatever his boss told him to, which included assassinations. The story my friend related was that the leader of a rival drug faction had kidnapped this guy's boss's granddaughter and had tortured the little girl for three days before finally killing her—all to send a message to the other cartel leader that he was in charge and not someone to cross. The guy we were looking at in this academic setting in Vermont was then ordered by his boss to do the same thing to the rival leader's grandson, which he did (according to my friend's story). He kidnapped the kid, tortured him for three days, and then killed him.

My friend (who claimed to know the guy), said that this killing was the turning point for the enforcer. That so pricked his conscience that he quit the biz and moved to the States and began a career as a writer. He'd written successful screenplays and was at that moment a vice president for a major television/motion picture studio, which I won't name for obvious reasons. Now, I have no way of verifying any of this, and it really doesn't matter if it's true or not, although I have no reason to doubt what was related to me. What I do know—and what's important to my story here—is that I recognized this guy as a bona fide dangerous man; and what's really important to the topic I began here (about story ideas and beginnings) is that the first line of a story popped into my mind at that instant, the afore-quoted:

> He was so mean that wherever he was standing became the bad part of town.

The story I eventually came up with was totally different from this guy's story, but what I came up with at that instant was a *character*, and not only a character, but a particularly original way of describing that character and creating an intriguing glimpse of him. A glimpse that would draw readers into the story because they'd simply have to know about such a man.

I think it worked. You be the judge.

Give the reader a character who's obviously cut out of different cloth than Everyman and you create a compelling opening.

———————————— 𝄐 ————————————

From Tim Sandlin's novel *Honey Don't*:

> RC Nash's sense of destiny was reignited by a flight attendant feeling bumps on his forehead.

You're not going to want to know about a character who's getting phrenology practiced on him by a stewardess on a plane? You're not going to want to know why she is feeling his noggin? Right ...

Have unique things happen to your character in ordinary situations, and you've intrigued the reader. The only caution in opening like this is to make sure that the action you give your character is related to the story that follows and isn't just some weird thing he is doing that has no real connection.

———————————— ⌾ ————————————

From Richard Brautigan's short story "A Need for Gardens":

> When I got there they were burying the lion in the back yard again.

The one word that makes this an opening that begs the reader to read further is *again.* They were burying the lion *again.* Even without this word, it would have been difficult to not read on—burying a lion in one's back yard isn't the most commonplace event in the universe, at least on our block—but when we learn that this isn't the first time they've buried this lion in the back yard, why wouldn't we want to plunge ahead and find out who *they* are, why they're burying a lion, why in the back yard, and why on earth *again*? A single, incongruent word like this can make the difference between a ho-hum opening and an intriguing one. Try picking up Brautigan's story seconds before you want to go to sleep for the night, and don't expect to be able to put it down and find out in the morning!

Hooked

From Pete Dexter's novel *Deadwood*:

> The boy shot Wild Bill's horse at dusk, while Bill was off
> in the bushes to relieve himself.

Well, hey, we know this is a book about Wild Bill Hick-
ok because that's what the cover promises, and we know
from even a limited knowledge of Old West lore that
Wild Bill was considered a violent kind of guy, so can
you imagine not wanting to find out what happens
to this kid when Bill returns from his whiz and finds
his horse dead and primed for the glue factory? If so,
you're a better man than I am, Charlie Brown.

Give your reader a tense situation like this, and
you're golden.

From Truman Capote's short story "Children on Their
Birthdays":

> Yesterday afternoon the six-o-clock bus ran over Miss
> Bobbit.

Notice anything about every single one of these openings?
They all promise trouble to come, show us trouble that's
already happened, or put us smack in the middle of trouble. Here, in Capote's story opening, aren't we dying to
know who Miss Bobbit is and what impact her getting run
over has on the protagonist/narrator's world? This opening is also a great example of specificity. It's not just a bus

that runs over Miss Bobbit, it's the six-o'clock bus. This is the same kind of opening as Brautigan's from "A Need for Gardens"—it depends on the inclusion of a single word to jar the reader's sensibility and interest him in what will follow. Try to think of ways to add a single word like this to an ordinary sentence and watch the magic that ensues.

───────────────── ∞ ─────────────────

From Harlan Coben's novel *The Final Detail*:

> Myron lay sprawled next to a knee-knockingly gorgeous brunette clad only in a Class-B-felony bikini, a tropical drink sans umbrella in one hand, the aqua clear Caribbean water lapping at his feet, the sand a dazzling white powder, the sky a pure blue that could only be God's blank canvas, the sun as soothing and rich as a Swedish masseur with a snifter of cognac, and he was intensely miserable.

Great opening! In the beginning of the opening sentence, we are lulled by the description of an idyllic situation and then, at the very end, Coben drops the bombshell, "and he was intensely miserable." The question instantly arises, how could this guy possibly be miserable in the middle of paradise? Will we have to read on to find out what makes him miserable? Of course! Exactly the response Coben desires. And guess what? Once again, there's trouble in Eden.

Create a beginning sentence or two describing something pleasurable, and then drop the forbidden apple into your Garden of Eden and wait for the acceptance letter from that agent or editor.

―――――――――――――――⎰⎱――――――――――――――

From Robert Crais's novel *Free Fall*:

> Jennifer Sheridan stood in the door to my office as if she were Fay Wray and I was King Kong and a bunch of black guys in sagebrush tutus were going to tie her down so that I could have my way.

Whoever Jennifer Sheridan is, she certainly promises to be a memorable character! As does the protagonist/narrator, who doesn't think in mundane or cliché metaphors. Employ metaphors that not only are original but fit the protagonist and the story like a tailored suit, and you're off to a great start to your story.

―――――――――――――――⎰⎱――――――――――――――

From Dennis Lehane's novel *A Drink Before the War*:

> My earliest memories involve fire.

If this guy's earliest memories involved Mom's chocolate chip cookies, would we be as intrigued? Don't think so. Fire is one of the most terrifying of natural elements in our world, and if you give your reader a character like this, whose earliest memories involve terror, and that terror is organic to the story that follows, well.... In real life, we want good things to happen to ourselves. In fiction, we need to seek out and portray the opposite.

Chapter Eight

From Maxine Hong Kingston's memoir, *The Woman Warrior*:

> "You must not tell anyone," my mother said, "what I am about to tell you."

Who can resist a secret? Especially one that looks to be possibly horrendous. Upon reading this sentence, most of us will bend forward, ears flexed, to hear what this secret is. Give your readers an opening that flatly states that somewhere in the text a secret will be revealed, a mystery unfolded, and you've hooked 'em.

This opening begins with dialogue, often a no-no. In this case it works because both participants are identified immediately and the context of the dialogue itself is crystal-clear.

From Joy Williams's story "Escapes":

> Bomber Boyd, age thirteen, told his new acquaintances that summer that his father had been executed by the state of Florida for the murder of a sheriff's deputy and his drug-sniffing German shepherd.

Lots of things going on here! The character's name, for starters. Who doesn't want to come along on a ride with a character named Bomber? Give your characters memorable and descriptive names and you can't lose. And, whose funny bone isn't tickled when the narrator delivers the fact that Bomber's father was executed for the murder not only of a lawman, but also of his dog? This opening is a classic example of establishing the rules of the story in the beginning. From the inclusion of the German shepherd bit, we know this isn't going to be a strictly serious story, but a black comedy instead. Williams has also woven a good bit of backstory and setup into this opening with "told his new acquaintances," which hints that either the character has moved (a traumatic experience in itself for a teenager), or that something else has happened that has forced him from his old circle of friends into new ones. Both interpretations indicate trouble in his life. This opening also shows that, in all likelihood, the protagonist's father is a drug dealer and a man who is no stranger to violence. Really look at this opening for the wealth of information it hints at with an economy of language. There are volumes spoken in just a single sentence. If you can deliver this degree of information in your opening sentence, the reader is going to embrace both you and your work and won't let go until the story's finished.

———————————————————⧖———————————————————

From Gabriel García Márquez's short story "Eva Is Inside Her Cat":

> All of a sudden she noticed that her beauty had fallen all apart on her, that it had begun to pain her physically like a tumor or a cancer.

Again, *trouble*. Not to be sexist, but I have a suspicion this will be especially enticing for women readers. Story questions raised? You betcha! We see immediately that there is going to be pain in this tale. Márquez has also chosen a universal theme—the beginning of death—which will appeal to both men and women readers. Create a protagonist who implies the universal by the particular and you've got a winner.

———————————— ∽ ————————————

From Tom Perrotta's short story "Forgiveness":

> Fifteen minutes before the opening kickoff of our '76 state championship game, Rocky DeLucca quit the football team.

Who is Rocky DeLucca (obviously a quintessential football player, with that nickname) and why did he quit minutes before the big game? I wanna find out, and I bet you do, too. Again, begin your story with a shocking development like this and you've solidly hooked your reader.

———————————— ∽ ————————————

From Richard Selzer's short story "Whither Thou Goest":

> "Brain-dead," said the doctor.

Here's one of those exceptions to the precept that you shouldn't begin stories with dialogue. However, if you'll recall, I did say that you can violate this rule if it's clear right away who's speaking and in what context, so the readers don't have to backtrack once they learn the players and the circumstances. We know a doctor is speaking (it says so), and we know what the words brain-dead mean without any explanation in such an instance. What we don't know is who the doctor is speaking to, who he is speaking of (who the patient is), and what impact the doctor's words are going to have on the recipient. We'll have to read on to find out the answers to those questions, won't we! If you opt to begin with dialogue, make sure it's clear from the git-go who's speaking and in what context, and you'll achieve an opening such as Selzer did.

———————————— ⌒ ————————————

From Jane Bradley's novel *Living Doll*:

> When my grandfather died he had a pair of my mother's panties in his pocket: white cotton, soft-worn from my mother's three-year-old girlish round butt.

Oh, boy. This signals serious trouble and some dark times ahead. This sure doesn't sound like Grandpa on *The Waltons*, does it! This is showing the reader the character of the protagonist's family and her background in just a few, well-chosen words. Again, this is the proper way to weave backstory and/or setup into your opening—with just a single image that speaks volumes.

———————————— ⌒ ————————————

From Tony Ardizzone's short story "My Mother's Stories":

> They were going to throw her away when she was a baby.

But obviously they didn't. Why? Or why not? Not only why didn't they throw her away, but why did they consider throwing her away? And, who were they? And, who is the object of their proposed action? There are lots of questions raised with this simple beginning sentence. When you open with questions like this that are begging to be answered, you've assured yourself of your reader's interest.

From Fran Gordon's novel *Paisley Girl*:

> Word has spread of my body, painted in the grotesque but of a shape more pleasing than that of any cafeteria-fed college girl.

Unless we've read the cover blurbs, we're not aware that the paint isn't really paint, but the manifestation of a rare form of leukemia that pigments the body in shapes resembling paisleys. Doesn't matter. Like many of us who slow down to watch the results of a car wreck, and are dying to know who was hurt or killed, how it happened, and all those kinds of things, readers are going to stop and watch this even if it is literal paint the protagonist is covered with. This is using a description to show the reader the trouble the protagonist faces. Again, story questions are raised, and they are questions based on something we don't see every day.

From Andre Dubus's short story "After the Game":

> I wasn't in the clubhouse when Joaquin Quintana went crazy.

But I bet we're going to hear about it, and I'll also bet we're going to want to hear all about it. A person going nuts is almost always interesting unless he lives with you or is a close neighbor. Give your reader a character who performs outrageous acts, and you've got him firmly on board.

———————————————— ⊗ ————————————————

From Michael Chabon's short story "A Model World":

> My friend Levine had only a few months to go on his doctoral dissertation, but when, one Sunday afternoon at Acres of Books, he came upon the little black paperback by Dr. Frank J. Kemp, he decided almost immediately to plagiarize it.

Uh oh. We've got a pretty good idea that nothing good is going to come of this, don't we? And that means we're going to have to read on to find out just what bad things are going to emanate from Levine's decision. Plant your character in the inner circle of bad things a-happenin', and you've earned your reader's interest.

———————————————— ⊗ ————————————————

From Mark Ray Lewis's short story "Scordatura":

> When you're seventeen and you're the gay son of a Baptist preacher from Dallas, Texas, and you have a lisp and a drawl and a musical gift and you were named Oral because an angel told your daddy to do so in a dream, then New York City can seem like it's saving your life.

Unless you've killed most of your brain cells by overusing demon rum or diet cola (or both), who among you can turn away from this opening and not want to know more about this guy and what's about to happen? A character with this many contradictions in his makeup is only capable of having extraordinary experiences. Open with a character like this and your reader isn't going to leave you, that's for certain! Again, as always, make certain that the trouble he's in isn't some unrelated bit of difficulty, but is a direct result of the character traits you've given him.

From John Updike's novel *Rabbit at Rest*.

> Standing amid the tan, excited post-Christmas crowd at the Southwest Florida Regional Airport, Rabbit Angstrom had a funny sudden feeling that what he has come to meet, what's floating in unseen about to land, is not his son Nelson and daughter-in-law Pru and their two children but something more ominous and intimately his: his own death, shaped vaguely like an airplane.

From Updike's marvelous *Rabbit* trilogy comes this intriguing opening. Not only the fans of his previous Rabbit novels, but new readers as well will want to know what's going to happen when this plane lands. Once again, trouble is clearly promised. Also, even though this is a novel late in a series, Updike doesn't begin with some kind of boring update as to what his character has been doing since the last novel, but opens instantly with trouble. Open with the promise of trouble, and then deliver trouble—in spades!

———————————————— ∞ ————————————————

That these openings all represent books and stories that were bestsellers and/or critically acclaimed is no surprise. With opening sentences like these, the manuscripts were sure to be read by agents and editors.

Look again at every single one of the openings presented here and you'll see they all have two things in common, no matter what story unfolds. First, they're all about one thing—*trouble.* Not a single benign, passive, nuttin'-happenin' opening in the bunch. They all promise a ride down uncharted, bumpy dirt roads to get to the final destination. Give us danger, trouble, an unsettled universe in your stories, just as these wonderful writers did, and your stories will have an excellent chance of achieving the same fate: publication.

The second thing each of these openings has in common is that each raises questions and provokes the reader's curiosity. In the final analysis, that's the main consideration to keep in mind when creating a hook. Make it so that the reader has no choice but to read the next sentence to find the answers to the mystery raised. All good stories, are, in a sense, mysteries. We read on to find out what happened. So give your future readers a mystery. Create a mystery in your opening that you promise to answer by the end of the book or story.

CHAPTER NINE

Red Flag Openers to Avoid

Now that we've gone over some great ways to open, here are a few approaches to avoid. While there are certainly more than the ones listed here, these five in particular seem to be the most commonly encountered by agents and editors in submissions; whenever they see one of these, a loud gong rings in their ears.

Don't ring the gong.

RED FLAG 1: OPENING WITH A DREAM

Never, ever, ever begin a narrative with action and then reveal the character's merely dreaming it all. Not unless you'd like your manuscript hurled across the room, accompanied by a series of curses. Followed by the insertion of a form rejection letter into your SASE and delivered by the minions of our illustrious postal service. Even though we're dealing with beginnings here, it bears mentioning that you should never—and I mean *never*—

end a story by revealing that all that has gone on before was just a dream. Not unless you enjoy the prospect of strangers hunting you down and doing you bodily harm should such a story somehow find print.

RED FLAG 2: OPENING WITH AN ALARM CLOCK BUZZING

Don't open with your protagonist waking to an alarm clock ringing, or to someone shaking her awake, or to a cute little birdie chirping from her bedroom window, or to a blazing sun shining through the window.

This is always a groaner for the agent or editor—a beginning in which she's introduced to the character waking up to an alarm clock ringing or to a clock radio announcing something important, such as that the Martians have landed. Such an opening signals clearly to the agent or editor that the writer is about to take her through a tedious and thoroughly dull journey of the character waking, eating breakfast, greeting all the numbingly boring children in the house, and so on. It's going to be hours before she gets to the actual story. Hours she's probably not going to invest.

The only thing worse than a story opening with a ringing alarm clock is when the character reaches over to turn it off and then exclaims, "I'm late!" I actually saw a movie in which that happened—wish I could remember the title so I could give it its deserved props.

Any intelligent reader will root for a cruel and unusual death for someone so irredeemably stupid as to set her alarm clock to go off late. After all, a character who sets her alarm clock so she'll be late and is then surprised when it goes off at the time she set it for may actually meet a person of the opposite sex who is equally brain damaged, and the scary thing is that they may have off-spring. Resulting in progeny from the shallow end of the gene pool. Now, that's a terrifying thought!

RED FLAG 3: BEING UNINTENTIONALLY FUNNY

Don't write sentences like: "Was she going to come in or stay out on the porch, he thought to himself." It's been fairly well verified down through the annals of history that when a human being thinks, he almost always does so to himself, and scarcely ever to another person, unless mind-reading is part of the story. When an editor encounters one of these kinds of sentences, your work is probably going to make her laugh, but that's not considered a positive reaction in this case.

RED FLAG 4: TOO LITTLE DIALOGUE

One of the primary red flags for many editors and agents is the absence of dialogue on the first few pages of a manuscript. All editors—no matter what the material, screenplay or novel or short story—look for lots and lots of nice white space. Some editors are even known to rifle the pages to see how dense the prose is. (Readers who cover screenplays do this automatically to check for the amount of dialogue in the script—there had better be a lot!) When fiction editors do this and see copy that isn't broken up much, it tells them one thing—that what they're about to encounter is likely to be narrative, narrative, and yet more narrative.

Signaling a read that promises to be boring.

And you know what that means.

Don't quit your day job just yet.

RED FLAG 5:
OPENING WITH DIALOGUE

This kind of opening was popular at the turn of the last century; it looks musty now. The problem with beginning a story with dialogue is that the reader knows absolutely nothing about the first character to appear in a story. For that matter, *any* of the characters. That means that when she encounters a line or lines of dialogue, she doesn't have a clue who the speaker is, who she is speaking to, and in what context. That requires that she read on a bit further to make sense of the dialogue. Then, at least briefly, she has to kind of backtrack in her mind to put it all into context. That represents, at the least, a speed bump, and at worst, a complete stall.

You don't want that! Your goal should be to write narratives with enough skill that the reader never has to pause to figure out what's going on. That interrupts the fictive dream the reader has willingly entered. Once the read is stalled, however momentarily, it becomes easy to put the story down. Many times, never to return. You want to avoid such stalls at all costs.

There are, of course, certain notable exceptions. A line like: "'I'd like to make love to Nancy,' Tom said to his pal Joey, 'but I'd have to look at her face to do it and I don't think I can do that.'" A dialogue opening like that may sometimes work. The thing is, if I began with a snatch of dialogue, I'd make certain that the meaning and context of the lines spoken were clear from the git-go.

Also, remember that a character's thoughts are a form of dialogue—they're an interior monologue. Just another reason to not open with the character ruminating.

Most times, if not always, look for a better way to begin your story than with dialogue.

CHAPTER TEN

Opening Scene Length and the Use of Transitions

Short or long? Which opening works best?

The answer is (envelope please) ... pause ... drum roll ... Short.

Deliver the inciting incident scene and then get right into the struggle to resolve the problem that incident has created. In other words, don't mess around. Get your protagonist in trouble right from the start.

Does this mean that the first *chapter* should be a short one? Not at all. That's the choice of the writer or editor. By *opening*, I'm referring only to the opening *scene* (dramatizing the inciting incident), which should, in most cases, be short; but it's perfectly acceptable to end that scene with a space break and continue at that point with the protagonist's first efforts to resolve the problem, or even to deliver a bit of necessary backstory. It's also okay to end the first chapter with the inciting incident scene, depending on how you want to structure the story. If, for example, the inciting incident is a particularly dramatic one, you might wish to make it the entire first chapter, even if it's a very short one, just to force the reader to pause a bit and consider what's just happened. Not to mention that ending a chapter after an unresolved dramatic scene is a proven page-turning technique. Leaving your character in severe straits is deliciously tension inducing, and it's a rare reader who can resist turning the page to chapter two. However, if your opening scene isn't *uber*-dramatic—perhaps your story calls for a seemingly smaller initial story problem that will eventually lead to one with much more at stake— then simply end the scene with a space break and continue with the chapter and subsequent developments. If you elect to use this technique, be sure that the rest of the chapter further embroils your character in increasing difficulties, and you'll ensure the reader's desire to go on to the next chapter.

One sure way to create shorter opening scenes is to eliminate most, if not all, the backstory that precedes the inciting incident. For instance, if you wish to write a story about a woman who wants to break free of a possessive relationship, you don't need to include all of the couple's history up to the point where she realizes she's entrapped. Most such relationships don't begin that way; they undergo a gradual metamorphosis during which one partner gradually tightens the noose. Keeping in mind that one of the requirements of an inciting incident is that it be an event that sets up the protagonist's eventual realization of story-worthy problem, the history leading up to that—no matter how important—doesn't belong in the inciting incident scene. That's all backstory, and while important, it doesn't belong here, but later on in the narrative.

In the current example, the scene that should begin the story is the one in which the possessive man hits the woman once too often, and it finally dawns on her that this abuse amounts to a kind of intolerable slavery. Perhaps a better opening scene in such a story might be when she tells him she wants to go downtown and get her driver's license and he tells her that she doesn't need such a thing; that if she needs to get somewhere he can take her, or a friend can, or she can even use a taxi or the bus. This scene would be dramatic, as opposed to the melodrama of a scene in which her partner strikes her. Perhaps all the beatings in the past, while horrible, never really drove home the fact that she's in a completely subservient role, but his refusal to allow her to get her driver's license is the straw that breaks the proverbial camel's back and clearly reveals to her for the first time the scope of her problem. All that backstory stuff—the beatings, the emotional and physical abuse, all of that—can be dealt out to the reader later on. Her desire to get a driver's license, his refusal of that request, and the impact of that refusal on her are all the ingredients of a first-class opening scene incorporating the inciting incident. And the scene will probably be relatively short. Somewhere between one and four pages would be ideal.

Chapter Ten

DETERMINING THE RIGHT LENGTH FOR A STORY OPENING

In a short story, which doesn't utilize chapters, a simple space break suffices if you're going to a new place after the inciting incident. If the story simply continues chronologically from that point, of course a space break isn't necessary.

In a novel, if your initial scene dramatizes a small beginning problem for the protagonist that will eventually lead to a much bigger problem as the story progresses, then it's not advisable to end the chapter after the smaller inciting incident. First chapters should end powerfully, leaving the character worse off than when the chapter began. Remember that part of the definition of an inciting incident is that it profoundly changes the protagonist's world and thereby creates a problem and also a goal (to resolve the problem). Ending the chapter after an incident that doesn't *appear* at this point to be that big of a deal may easily signal (incorrectly) to the reader that this is as bad as it will get, and after reading a fairly mild beginning and seeing the apparently small inciting incident at the end of chapter one, your reader may get the impression that your story isn't going to be that exciting of a read.

A good example of such a relatively benign opening can be found in Jim Harrison's novella *Brown Dog*, the first of the three novellas in his book *The Woman Lit by Fireflies*. *Brown Dog* begins with this paragraph:

> Just before Dark at the bottom of the sea I found the Indian. It was the inland sea called Lake Superior. The Indian, and he was a big one, was sitting there on a ledge of rock in about seventy feet of water. There was a frayed rope attached to his leg and I had to think the current had carried him in from deeper water. What few people know is that Lake Superior stays so cold near the bottom that drowned bodies never make it to the surface. Bodies don't rot and bloat like in other fresh water, which means they don't make the gas to carry them up to the top. This fact upsets working sailors on all sorts of ships. If the craft goes down in a storm their loved ones will never see them again. To me this is a stupid worry. If you're dead, who cares? The point here is the Indian, not death. I wish to God I had never found him. He could have drowned the day before if it hadn't been for his eyes, which were missing.

While interesting, at this point the opening is fairly benign. The narrator's obviously not related to the dead man, so there's no personal loss here, and nothing indicates that the Indian is anything more than a stranger whose body he's come across. The only hint that this incident is going to be important enough to rock his world is in the sentence where the narrator simply tells us it's a big deal: "I wish to God I had never found him." We'll see later that finding this body in Lake Superior is going to change his life for ever, but that's really not evident at this point.

Therefore, if Harrison had ended his opening here and labeled it chapter one, or even if he followed it with a space break, the reader might well have concluded that this was a Peggy Lee opening (from her signature song, "Is That All There Is?"). Harrison didn't, though. Instead, Harrison segues organically from this opening paragraph into informing the reader that the narrator is transcribing his discovery to a lover. He then delivers some necessary backstory, moving from that into how the discovery of the dead man begins to impact the narrator's life.

The point is, if you have a Peggy Lee kind of opening, don't make it a chapter by itself! Deliver at least a bit more of the song, and end on a more dire note.

As for an example of a short opening scene dramatic enough to serve also as the entire first chapter, well, to be honest, I couldn't find one. I searched through close to four hundred novels to find such an opening, and failed to locate any. I'm sure they're out there, but I couldn't find even one! In almost all cases, however, the opening scene itself was fairly short, no matter the quality of the scene. Most only took an average of one to four pages to relate, even though the rest of the chapter was quite lengthy. There are some opening chapters that are *relatively* short—several I read that were three to four pages typeset—but none that were only a few paragraphs. That should probably tell us that, while there's nothing inherently wrong with short beginning chapters (chapters that are one to two pages in length), it's probably best to make 'em a bit longer. That said, and to quote an old chestnut that happens to be true most times, rules are made to be broken, and if you feel a shorter opening chapter works for your story, go for it.

WHAT ANY OPENING—LONG OR SHORT—REQUIRES

The primary requirement of an opening is that the first line plunges the reader into the story instantly. A slow, leisurely beginning is just not acceptable to readers these days, unless you're a brand-name author whose fans will pick up anything and everything you write, or unless the book you're working on is any but the first in a series. In both cases, waiting fans may be predisposed to wade through a lethargic opening; other books and stories won't be granted a similar amount of patience by the reader. And while a slow beginning may sometimes be acceptable in a novel, rarely will such a beginning be tolerated in a short story.

So, what's the proper length for a story opening? The answer is: As short as you can make it.

Open the story, show readers the problem via a scene, and then have your character get to work on the problem.

That's it, pretty much.

Short and sweet does the work best.

USING TRANSITIONS TO ANCHOR YOUR OPENING SCENES

Regardless of length, opening scenes aren't standalone chunks of writing. To work properly, they have to lead into the rest of the story as effortlessly as possible, so as not to cause the reader to hesitate or even completely stall. That means you need to create transitions that are as seamless as possible.

Transitions have come a long way from the earliest days of writing, even more so in the past few years. To understand how these changes have come about, let's look at the film industry. Movies are not only illustrative of how transitions have changed; they are actually largely responsible for the way transitions in fiction are written nowadays.

Way back in the mists of time (the early 1900s), when silent movies were being produced, transitions in those films were made pretty much like transitions in the written work—with a direct and glaring notice to the movie patron. Print would scroll on the scene any time the movie was getting ready to go to another place or time in the narrative. Something in Caligula script would scroll across the otherwise blank background: MEANWHILE, BACK AT THE RANCH ... Look at some of those old movies, like *The Birth of a Nation*, for instance, and you'll see what I mean.

Novels did the same thing when transitioning to a new place or time period. High school English teachers spent weeks and months teaching fledgling writers to create great transition sentences and to use various transition techniques to transport the reader hither and yon: flashbacks and flashforwards and location changes, or focusing on another character, as the story required. Movies just borrowed those same techniques. In those days, since film was new, movies borrowed just about everything from literature as far as story technique was concerned.

The same thing happened when movies incorporated sound. Now, producers could substitute a voice-over for the text transition, interchange the two techniques, or even use both to *really* let the viewers know they were going to a new place or time. Movie people were still borrowing from literature, even with the added benefit of sound.

Now, it's the other way around. Movies long ago passed literature in many aspects of craft and aesthetics, and it is the norm nowadays for fiction writers—as well as writers in almost all other forms—to borrow from what is being shown at the local cineplex. Some embrace the new techniques in their writing careers; some fight 'em. Fighting these techniques is kind of like battling a tsunami with a bucket, in my opinion, but, hey, do whatever you think best. Resisters may change their minds after reading this section. Change isn't a bad thing, by the way. Remember: When you're green, you're growing; when you're ripe, you're rotten.

A sea of change occurred in relation to transitions in 1960 with the release of French director Jean-Luc

Godard's first film, *Breathless.* Godard changed forever the way both movies and literature were structured; he invented a transitional technique called the jump cut.

A jump cut is just what it sounds like it is. The narrative of the film simply jumps to the next scene without forewarning the viewer.

Like so many of civilization's innovations, the new method Godard employed came about because of financial expediency.

He'd overshot the film—he'd shot eight thousand meters of film, and the producer required a maximum of five thousand meters. Godard had to cut the film down so it would be financially viable to run in theaters and, therefore, obtain a distributor. Then, as now, money ran the show. It would be nice to say that artistic concerns are what create innovations, but often as not, it's the CPAs of the world who initiate progress.

Here is Godard's own explanation of what happened, from his *Introduction á une véritable histoire du cinéma*:

> [W]hen we came to this sequence, which had to be shortened like the others, instead of slightly shortening both, the editor and I flipped a coin; we said: "Instead of slightly shortening one and then slightly shortening the other, and winding up with short little shots of both of them, we're going to cut out four minutes by eliminating one or the other altogether, and then we will simply join the [remaining] shots, like that, as though it were a single shot."

Thus was born the jump cut. At first, there was wide-spread resistance and critical panning of the new method. Isn't there always? It's hard for old dogs to learn new tricks, especially if one has spent years learning the familiar tricks. It's no different today. There are still many teachers standing before classes, introducing units on how to write transitions such as "Jeremy thought back to the first day he had visited Aunt Mabel on that fateful day in ..." and never mentioning there's a new wrinkle out there (well, *new* if you consider 1960 to be a recent year).

Even though there was considerable resistance to what Godard had done with his jump cuts, there was also a bunch of film folks who thought Godard's transitions were kind of neat, and eventually, the new kids on the block ruled.

Eventually, the screen direction *jump cut* was even included in screenplay software such as Final Draft and Movie Magic Screenwriter, although jump cuts have been utilized for so long, to insert one into a script nowadays is considered kind of boneheaded and more than a bit archaic. Screenwriters don't even employ the term in their scripts any longer, for fear of coming across as newbies. These days, even the term *jump cut* is considered a bit archaic and it is therefore avoided. Screenwriters just write the next scene without any labeling, regardless of its placement in the narrative, chronological or not.

Kind of like what Christopher Moore does in *Island of the Sequined Love Nun*, remember? He transitions from the present of the story—the inciting incident scene that begins the novel—to a flashback of an event that occurred several months previous without even a space break to signal it. He just goes back in the middle of a sentence, albeit with language that indicates a flashback is beginning.

The jump cut has also largely done away with dissolves and wipes, both vestiges of old-fashioned literary transitions. They still exist, but aren't used in nearly the same numbers as they were years ago, and they are rapidly disappearing. Another movie transition technique—also borrowed from literature—is one a director such as John Ford would use. He'd begin with a wide panoramic shot of a scene—say a sweeping shot of a grand prairie with majestic mountains in the background—and then keep narrowing the subsequent shots down, until the focus was on an individual standing next to a buck wagon. Maybe he would even narrow the view all the way down to the top half of the cowboy's face, with the eyes doing a bit of glaring-at-the-bad-guy acting. Oscar stuff, you know.

This was directly taken from now-archaic literary technique in which the author would begin with an overview of the entire eastern seaboard of the U.S., say, then work down bit by bit to a small particular scene in which a guy pulls a gun from his jacket pocket. Descriptive scenes that go on forever—from a wide shot to a small particular one—are long gone from literature as well as from films. At least from books that find their way to bookstore shelves.

These days, moviegoers don't even think about the way movies go from scene to scene without any buildup or forewarning. We're just suddenly there. Today's audiences "get it" and are used to experiencing movies this way. Book readers have been trained by movies and novels that do the same kinds of transitions (read: *no* transitions), and they "get it" just as readily.

In 1994, Quentin Tarantino was hailed by moviegoers and critics as an innovator for the manner in which he played with the traditional chronological narrative in his film *Pulp Fiction*. Actually, it wasn't an innovation as much as a natural progression from what Godard began.

Now, if we can just convince writing teachers to discover these innovations in transitions and adapt their teaching lessons to the new reality. Even if they don't entirely get rid of units on transitions, they may at least restructure them or cut down the amount of time spent on such lessons.

Look at movies to figure out where writing is or should be going. Film and television are doing the most in training readers these days. The astute writer will realize that and write accordingly. I wouldn't spend a lot of time designing lap covers for passengers in unheated Model Ts when most of today's cars come equipped with perfectly good heaters.

CHAPTER ELEVEN

The View From the Agent's and Editor's Chair

Listen to what the gatekeepers in publishing have to say about story beginnings. I'd listen very carefully—these are the folks who decide the fate of your manuscript! I posed a series of questions to agents and editors, and will recount their feedback in this chapter.

But first, before we get to what these folks have to say, let's take a look at how we arrived at the story structure considered marketable today, particularly the structure of story openings.

Beginnings have changed more than any other part of story structure. Many millennia had to pass before we got to where we are today. Most of the changes have taken fairly lengthy periods of time to achieve. Except the most recent. The most profound changes have taken place in a relatively short period. Mostly during the age of television and movies and modern communication (computers, telephones, etc.) and the resultant shifts in the way we perceive information and entertainment. Our world is shrinking. Our collective attention span shrinks with it as the universe speeds up, bombarding us with more and more information. And more and more entertainment options.

Books have to change or get lost in the mix.

The truth is, many books *are* getting lost in the mix, and this is largely due to the fact that there are still writers churning out a product written in a style and with a structure my son Mike would most likely describe as being "So five minutes ago."

The biggest changes have come about primarily because of TV and movies. Those two methods of delivering drama into our lives have changed the landscape of storytelling forever.

Think about this: How many people do you know who watch television and movies, but who read very little or not at all? How many people do you know who only read and never watch television or movies? I'll wager the second figure is far smaller than the first. In fact, you may not even be able to come up with a single acquaintance that hasn't watched TV or seen a movie. That should tell you something of the influence of these two media.

Fifty years ago, and certainly seventy-five years ago, the opposite would have been true. Seventy-five years is a relatively short period of time, as civilization and mankind go, yet the most cataclysmic changes to story have occurred in that sliver of time.

That means our older models of writing stories have changed and changed drastically. If we're still following the story structure models of the world before World War II, or before the Vietnam War era, for instance, we may be hopelessly out of date. In fact, we almost certainly are!

Even the things we read as a society have changed. Nonfiction outsells fiction about ten to one. I'll bet you know at least several acquaintances who claim they never read fiction these days. The reason given is usually along the lines of "I'd like to read fiction, but I just don't have time. I have to spend what little time I do have on information I need for my job." What that means to us as fiction writers is that we have to be even better at what we do than our novelist forebears were. We have to pay even more attention to the structure of our stories if we expect people to give up their precious time to read them.

The impact to story structure is this: Those novels of yesteryear—the so-called classics or novels of any stripe of those days—could be leisurely or slowly developed stories.

But today, as boxer Roberto Durán infamously said, in what turned out to be a bad day at the office for him, "No más, no más."

THE POWER OF BOOKSCAN

A factor in what determines which books sell to publishers and which books don't is the recent and rapid advent of the service called Nielsen BookScan, which began in Australia and now encompasses the United States and England as well, with the aim of covering pretty much the entire book-buying market worldwide. BookScan provides weekly reports on which books are actually selling in the bookstores by obtaining and compiling the information from bookstore cash registers. Because it doesn't depend on unconfirmed reports or a publisher's PR spin of what's selling and what's not, BookScan provides an accurate and timely report of the true state of sales.

BookScan has revealed the decline of what is usually referred to as literary fiction. This category of fiction may be dying because it has stuck with the story structure model of yesteryear much more so than has any other category. While this may not be the entire reason literary fiction sales are lagging, evidence suggests strongly that it's a major contributing factor. Publishers pay attention to BookScan and take its statistics into account when purchasing manuscripts, which means that agents do so as well. What that means to today's writers—like it or not—is that their stories are going to have a far greater chance of selling if they adhere to the current popular taste in fiction, as reflected by the sobering statistics BookScan provides. Languorous, leisurely openings won't cut it these days.

As Michael Webster, the publishing insider who initially introduced the book sales tracker BookScan to Australian publishing, says, "I think [BookScan] is forcing publishers to see themselves as an industry. It's bringing that cold, hard commercial side into it." Melbourne author and academic Mark Davis says BookScan has been a boon for mass-market fiction, a killer for literary fiction. Almost overnight, BookScan has replaced the publisher's and publicist's spin and hype with statistics, and eliminated the traditional delays in reporting actual sales.

This means that booksellers know within days which titles are moving and which are collecting dust, and you'd better know that publishers are going to have to pay attention, whether they want to or not. Most will; they're in business for the same reason anyone else is—to make money, not to serve as altruistic patrons of art.

PUBLISHING: AN EVOLVING INDUSTRY

As a culture, we've been trained to receive stories visually by movies and television since at least the fifties. The same holds true of literature—because of our experience with movies, we now expect to be plunged instantly into the "action" of the story on the page just as we are plunged into the action on the screen. No longer will we sit still for languorous openings to our written stories—the visual arts have taught us something must happen right from Jump Street. Stories today had better be wound tight and delivered quickly. They can't begin any longer with pages of backstory and setup. To be considered publishable, they have to begin with action and with the trouble that's going to occupy the story. You may not like this news, but it's true and there's very little anyone can do about it.

Oh, sure, you can continue to write those kinds of old-fashioned passive novels in which thirty pages go by with nothing but great globs of description or summary, but who's going to read it? Certainly not the reading public, because those kinds of books simply stand little, if any, chance of publication; and if somehow they do find print, not many people are going to plunk down their hard-earned cash for such books.

Even a relatively few short years ago, some publishers were willing to put out such books in hopes of snagging one of those prestigious literary prizes. That isn't done nearly as much these days. They've discovered not enough people buy 'em. And it's all about the bottom line today. The midlist of former years just doesn't exist any more. Publishers have discovered it doesn't help keep them in business to nurture a writer and absorb losses on a writer's early work, solely in the hope that future books will prove profitable. Most publishers these days expect a book to at least show the potential to become a bestseller. It's that kind of mentality that permeates publishing today and can one really blame publishers? It's all well and good to be the kind of publisher that looks at art for art's sake, but while that might be a noble sentiment, it doesn't pay the rent or the salaries of the editors or the utility bills. And publishers are no different than any of us individuals. If we don't make more money than we spend, we're either going to switch to another line of work or become homeless.

What we refer to as mainstream or literary fiction represents a rapidly shrinking market. The fiction market today is being driven by genres. A book needs to fit a category to make it most of the time.

Just this past weekend (May 6, 2006 for anyone who happens to be curious), I walked into our local Borders bookstore and discovered that the whole place had changed. Before that last visit, easily the largest section in the store had been devoted to general fiction. That means mainstream or literary fiction, and any fiction that isn't easily categorized under a particular genre.

Last Saturday, the Border's gnomes, no doubt working in the wee hours of the morning, had drastically reduced the amount of shelf space devoted to general fiction. It was maybe a third of its former size. They'd also tripled the size of the section where the thrillers and mysteries sleep. Tripled it! They'd also added a brand-new and very large section of greeting cards and gifts where much of the general fiction had once been housed.

I imagine this wasn't an isolated case. I would dare say the same thing is happening to many, if not all of the Borders bookstores nationwide. Why the change?

Money. Profit. Bookstores operate on a very low margin of profit. Take it from me—I've owned two bookstores and the next time I want to lose my shirt I'll just pour my money down a hole. It'll take longer to disappear that way than it would if I invested in a bookstore.

The state of publishing and selling books is somewhat like the state farming used to be in. Which reminds me of a story ...

A few years ago, when corn and soybean prices had fallen to all-time lows, a local farmer saw a hardware store offering a sale on padlocks. Dollar apiece. He got an idea. Went in to the hardware and bought ten thousand locks. His plan was to sell them for two dollars and make a good profit. As it happened, there wasn't much of a market for padlocks and he ended up having to get rid of all of them at fifty cents apiece.

When he'd sold the last of them, he went back to the hardware store and ordered ten thousand more. The store owner, who'd kept himself apprised of the farmer's difficulties in moving the merchandise, said, "You want more? I heard you had to sell that other batch for half of what you paid for them."

The farmer said, "Well, sir, that I did. But, all in all, it's sure more profitable than farming!"

That's kind of where bookselling is today. Which is why the mainstream or literary section is being reduced. Those books don't sell as well as genre books. They don't even seem to sell as well as cute little greeting cards and rolls of wrapping paper. Many of those books are being written in a style that's gone out of vogue, with leisurely beginnings (and middles and endings), and stories that spend an awful lot of time with the protagonist/narrator ruminating instead of actually *doing* stuff. Many of these books seem more like fictionalized memoirs, but unfortunately, not memoirs about anybody who ever did anything interesting, unless you consider conjugating verbs in Midwestern classrooms for bored students, who will turn out to be as insipid as the adults, the stuff of great drama.

That's the bad news. The good news is that Borders has beefed up their sections featuring genres. That indicates a healthy market for the folks who write those kinds of books.

Like you, publishers have little desire to become homeless or find themselves in an unemployment line. The market demands a different kind of novel today, and it's the publisher's job to deliver what the market wants. Which means it's our job as writers to deliver that kind of book if we expect to see it on the shelves at the bookstore. I don't mean to overstate this, but there seem to be too many people who keep thinking they will be able to return to some kind of Golden Age of Literature, and that's just not going to happen.

It's important to grasp that and get on with a writing life that has a chance of succeeding. Makes sense, doesn't it?

Here's something else to consider. For every statement made here about the kinds of books currently in vogue and the methods of writing publishable material these days (especially as pertains to story beginnings), one might (and probably can) find examples that belie the statement. There are exceptions to everything! However, if you can't find more than a very few such exceptions, you might ask yourself if you want to stake your writing career on those few who achieve print against the current wisdom. To do so would be almost like arranging your fortune in life by walking the same path, step for step, as did the man who was struck by lightning on his way to purchase his winning lottery ticket. You may feel it's worth getting hit by the lightning to get the ten-million-dollar prize. If so, all I can do is wish you good luck!

However, one of the purposes of this book is to point out some of the roadblocks to publication most writers will face, so that you can avoid them. Some people overcome roadblocks on their way to their goal, but do you really want to play in a poker game with a pair of deuces against five other players who've stayed through the last draw? Sometimes deuces win, sure. But mightn't you have a better chance of winning the pot if you waited to go all in until you were holding four aces?

AGENTS AND EDITORS SPEAK OUT ON BEGINNINGS

Here's what the guys and gals who have the power to say "yea" or "nay" to you manuscript have to say on the subject of story beginnings. Pay attention—these folks have the power over the future of your novel. I posed a series of questions to agents and editors, and this is how they replied.

What, in your opinion, is the single biggest mistake writers make in their story beginnings?

Jodie Rhodes, President, Jodie Rhodes Literary Agency

When it comes to selling your book, the most important words you'll ever write are those on page one. Unless you grab our attention immediately, your book has no chance.

Countless writers have told me (often vehemently) that their book gains power as it goes along, that it really gets exciting once a reader gets into it, so please give it the chance it deserves.

That will never happen and you just have to accept it. I receive almost 1,500 queries and manuscript submissions a month, and the large agencies receive considerably more. Time is our most precious commodity. We never have enough of it. So if you want to interest us, you've got to do it on page one. Keep in mind that editors operate just like we do. If they're not captivated by the words on page one, off goes the rejection.

Consider this: If you go on a blind date and have zero interest in the person you've met, would you agree to see them a second time?

Mike Farris, Farris Literary Agency, Inc.

We see two fairly common mistakes. The first is the beginning that isn't really a beginning of the story but is simply the backstory or static introduction of the character.

These openings usually consist of multiple pages of narrative, none of which move the story forward or get it started. Sometimes they even go backwards—"As John looked out over the vast expanse of wilderness, he thought back to how he had gotten there. Two years earlier he had …"

The other mistake is the effort to hook the reader with something exciting that turns out to have nothing whatsoever to do with the story. Explosions and murders can be exciting, but if they don't get the current story started, leave them out.

Toni Weisskopf, Publisher, Baen Books

Not clearly identifying a point-of-view character's particulars. I need to know fairly soon, in the first few paragraphs, if the narrator or viewpoint character is male or female, young or old, sophisticated or innocent. The fallback assumption from the reader is that the sex of the viewpoint character is the same as that of the writer; if it's going to be different, the reader needs to know right away.

After that, too many would-be writers assume an interest in what's going on from the reader they haven't earned yet. I can't be interested in a character crying or a character in peril if I don't know that character yet.

Julie Castiglia, Castiglia Literary Agency

The story should begin on the first page, but often it doesn't, so there is no reason to read on. Give us a reason to turn that page. Never ever start with weather, dreams, setup, or a passive scene that takes the reader nowhere.

Janet Reid, Literary Agent, JetReid Literary Agency

Opening statically, not dynamically. Description of just about anything instead of movement. Opening with the weather, a dream, a prologue with a character ruing the day s/he got involved with whatever.

Anonymous Senior Editor, Farrar, Straus and Giroux

Every bad beginning is bad in its own special way.

> *This was contributed by a senior editor at Farrar, Straus and Giroux, who asked to remain unnamed, as he or she very wisely didn't want to be inundated with submissions of books with bad beginnings.

Bob Silverstein, President, Quicksilver Books Literary Agents

Front-loading of information. Too much tell, not enough show.

Barbara Collins Rosenberg, Literary Agent

Writers tend to begin with the backstory and also overload the reader with details and descriptions of the characters.

What do you consider to be strong beginnings to stories and novels?

Jodie Rhodes, President, Jodie Rhodes Literary Agency

So how do you make your opening page a grabber? Let's start with some things you should not do.

Never open with scenery! Novels are about people, about the human condition. That's why we read them. Yet writer after writer starts off with descriptions of cities, towns, streets, forests, mountains, oceans, etc. Of course I know why. They've learned how to describe landscapes in language that seems literary, and hope we'll be impressed. We are not. We are looking for life.

Never open with the villain if you're doing mysteries, thrillers, suspense, horror, science fiction, or fantasy genres. If you're writing any novel that has a villain, do not open with him or her. In addition to looking for life, we are looking for voice. Nothing is more important to us than the voice of the protagonist. That is what drives a novel. So give us the protagonist up front.

Yes, I know many bestselling authors open with the villain doing his ghastly deed. Once you're a bestseller, you can do pretty much what you want until readers stop buying your books. The other thing is, these authors are usually writing series, so the reader is already acquainted with the protagonist. You don't have any of this going for you. In addition, most amateur (meaning unpublished) writers horribly bungle the characters of villains, creating boring and often ridiculous stereotypes.

Mike Farris, Farris Literary Agency, Inc.

Strong beginnings start in the middle of the story. You can fill in backstory later. I like to see the protagonist in action at the start so that I get a feel for who the character is right off the bat. We often get submissions with cover letters that begin: "I know you asked for the first fifty pages, but the story doesn't really get going until page 57, so I included more." If the story doesn't really get going until page 57, you probably need to cut the first 56 pages.

Julie Castiglia, Literary Agent

[A story] must begin with an immediate hook. Go to some of the classics to see how to begin, namely, *A Tale of Two Cities*, by Charles Dickens; *Offshore*, by Penelope Fitzgerald; *Pride & Prejudice*, by Jane Austen; *Madame Bovary*, by Gustave Flaubert. That first sentence and paragraph immediately draws one into the story and makes it impossible for the reader not to read on.

Anonymous Senior Editor, Farrar, Straus and Giroux

From three of our most recent books: "There were no books when I was a boy. Books were hardly accessible, yet there were some books." From author Sheila Heti in *Ticknor*. "Here's a red and white VW van, parked and baking in the sun on this clear and warm May day, and the young woman seated in the front passenger seat, the van's sole occupant, stirs uncomfortably, her clothes sticking to her, her scalp roasting under the towering Afro wig she wears. She is, she hopes, inconspicuous." From author Christopher Sorrentino in *Trance*. "Surprised? Of course I was surprised." From Etgar Keret's *Fatso*.

Janet Reid, Literary Agent

Action. Danger. Conflict. Crisis. Consider this from Jeff Somers's *The Electric Church* (forthcoming from Warner Aspect Books): "You fucked up Mr. Cates." Do we know who Mr. Cates is? No. Do we know what he looks like or where he is? No, but we will. What we know *now* is that he's in trouble. Of course I want to read on.

Bob Silverstein, Literary Agent

An immediate connection between author and reader ... a sense of something vital at stake.

Toni Weisskopf, Publisher, Baen Books

Almost anything can make a strong beginning: a well-turned phrase, an interesting characterization, a new way of looking at the familiar, an exciting circumstance. It's all in the way an author reveals his voice and the style of the story, very much like an introduction to a song. It can be done a million different ways, but has to give the listener an idea of what to expect from the rest of the music.

Jacky Sach, Co-founder, Bookends Literary Agency

[This book opening] sold me immediately:

> Sterling remembered Lara, the first time he'd noticed her. He saw the vision clearly, like she was right there across from him now instead of the police captain with

his basset hound face and red-rimmed eyes. (From Jennifer Patrick's *The Night She Died*)

Barbara Collins Rosenberg, Literary Agent

I tend to like books that start in the middle of a scene. I
want to be involved in the action right away.

HOW IMPORTANT DO YOU CONSIDER STORY BEGINNINGS TO BE, AND WHY?

Mike Farris, Farris Literary Agency, Inc.

Strong beginnings are of critical importance because,
without a strong beginning, the reader has no incen-
tive to read further. There are too many things competing for a reader's attention; you have to hook the reader
right up front with something—a compelling character,
a critical situation, or incredible writing. Make it worth
the reader's while to continue.

Julie Castiglia, Literary Agent

Enormously important. If the beginning is boring, why
read on? When you go to the bookstore, don't you immediately look at the first page of a book to see if you
even want to buy it? I have in a few cases removed the first
chapter before sending [the manuscript] to the publisher.

Janet Reid, Literary Agent

When I look at a book in the bookstore, I open it to the
first page and read for maybe five seconds. If it doesn't

get me involved in that very short amount of time, I set it back down and look at something else. Readers don't go to bookstores with lists of shoulds: Oh, I should buy this author, he worked hard; I should buy this book cause it's just as good as that other one. Book buyers buy books they want to read. Thus, as an agent, I look for books that will make that connection. It's hard to over-emphasize the importance of a good beginning.

Toni Weisskopf, Publisher, Baen Books

As Mr. Edgerton posits, without interesting the first reader at the publisher's house, the story won't ever see the light of day. Beginnings *must* be strong.

Bob Silverstein, Literary Agent

The first few paragraphs are crucial in letting the reader know that he or she is in authoritative hands. It's all about storytelling.

Anonymous Senior Editor, Farrar, Straus and Giroux

If one sentence is crummy, why would sentence two be any good?

Barbara Collins Rosenberg, Literary Agent

The beginning is crucial. I sometimes stop reading manuscripts, and yes, even published books, after only three or so pages.

Chapter Eleven

I am including the opening first page of several novels that not only hooked me but editors.

The first is not one of my authors but I am so impressed with Ken Follet's opening words in *The Key to Rebecca* that I quote it here to show you what wonders the right sentence can accomplish.

"The last camel collapsed at noon." In six words, the author has evoked an exotic place and a highly dangerous situation. Who could resist reading on?

Debra Seely wrote a young adult novel titled *Grasslands* that was won in auction by Holiday House, with Henry Holt the runner-up, and has garnered starred reviews and several awards. She intrigued me with her first sentence, "The letter came to my grandparents' house while I was at school in a fistfight."

Ann Pearlman was one of my first authors. Her book *Infidelity* mesmerized me on page one. MacAdam/Cage brought it out hardcover and a heated auction for paperback rights involving twelve publishers was won for $250,000 by Broadway. Hodder bought the rights in the U.K. and the London *Observer* serialized the book in their Sunday magazine, with the author's photo on the cover. Lions Gate optioned the movie rights and the movie debuted on Lifetime last April and is still being rerun.

> David is eleven months old and sits on the floor, not yet able to walk. His toys are helter-skelter around him. Toys that were once mine. I am three and I hate him.

Maggie Martin's debut novel, *Diagnosis of Love*, is another perfect example of hooking the reader on page one. Random House, Penguin, Warner, and HarperCollins all wanted the book. Bantam won it with a two-book offer.

> I'm nervous for several reasons as we hurtle down Route 70 in the pouring rain. I'm nervous about the wet road, the speeding obstacles on it, and my Volvo's faulty steering, which is making me swerve back and forth between the roadlines. I'm even more nervous because the last person on earth that I want to be doing me a favor— the controlling demanding Dr. Mary Worthington—is making hospital rounds in the ICU this morning so that I could get an early start on our road trip.
>
> Then there's the real reason my palms are clammy and my heart keeps turning over: I'm afraid that Mama isn't going to show up. I'm scared this whole adventure may be a failure. *Meet me there, Mama*, I silently pray, gripping the clumsy steering wheel.

Kathleen Coskran won my heart with her opening sentence and I could hardly wait to read the rest of the manuscript, *Waiting for James Taylor*. The book is now under consideration by several publishers.

> People don't climb major mountains like Mount Kenya carrying a valise. I know that now. Wouldn't have done it that way if I'd had a choice, but I didn't have money for a backpack, didn't have money for a sleeping bag, didn't have money for much but a kilo of rice and a box

225

of raisins. It was food enough for the five days I'd be on the mountain. I'd planned to spend the night in the top hut until a steely-eyed German in black spandex offered me a sleeping bag, which I nearly took until I realized he would be in it. I wanted to be warm, but not that warm.

The first page of Dominica Radulescu's *Train to Trieste* literally enchanted me so much that I sprang up from the dinner table where I was eating with one hand and opening the day's pile of submissions with the other and ran to the computer to send her an e-mail. The manuscript is now on submission with editors.

I am returning from the Black Sea wild and disheveled, my skin golden and salty and my hair entangled and blonder from the sun. A girl I used to know has just died on a hiking accident in the mountains: she was hit in the head by a rock on a trip with her boyfriend. He had accidentally sent down that rock, as he was walking behind her, on the steep path. I see him going in circles and smoking unfiltered Romanian cigarettes, the worst cigarettes in the world, bitter and sour, and as I watch him, suddenly my heart aches and pines for him.

There is no meat in the stores and no toilet paper, and flour, oil and sugar are rationed. People say it's about as bad now as it was during Stalinism. The worst of it all is that there are men in black leather jackets with small squinting eyes who watch and listen at every corner, on every floor of every building, on every telephone line, in every line for cheese or chicken wings, to see if you are complaining, if you make a joke, if you plan to leave the country, if you speak with foreigners, and to know where you got your Kent cigarettes from.

But this summer when I am seventeen and returning from the Black Sea, I am bursting into being a woman and I don't care about empty stores and sugar and flour rations. All I care about is that this man grieving for his dead lover turn his eyes on me.

Suzanne Phillips, a first-time writer with no credentials (the very hardest writer in the world to sell) sent me sample chapters of her novel, *Chloe Doe*. In my marketing letter to editors I attached the opening five pages. Seventeen U.S. editors and ten U.K. editors responded immediately, requesting the complete manuscript. Little, Brown and Company won the book here, MacMillan won it in the U.K., and it's already sold in Italy, Germany, and Holland. Below, the words on page one.

This is the Place You Become Miss America.

At four P.M. the music plays in rec. This is where we learn a new talent. We will all learn dance or it's back to our rooms for solitude, to think about why we don't want to learn the meringue, to think about why we don't want to hold the sweaty, fat hand of Dolores or Tina, why we don't want to swing across the floor in the arms of one of our own. They want us to say we were no good but now that's changed.

Chapter Eleven

The first question they ask you the first time they pick you up: Where are you from? The time before now. The time when you had parents and maybe brothers and sisters. Where did you live?

How old are you?

Eighteen.

You're not eighteen. Do you have proof you're eighteen? Show me proof you're eighteen, and this time I let you walk.

Jacky Sack, Co-founder, Bookends Literary Agency

It depends on the type of book, but I represent a great deal of mystery and believe a strong beginning is necessary to hook the reader immediately. We readers have a lot of competition for our time these days and need a reason to keep on reading. However, ultimately, it's the quality of the writing that snags me.

ADDITIONAL ADVICE AND COMMENTS TO WRITERS

Janet Reid, Literary Agent

When you write, don't obsess about the beginning. Write the whole novel, then look at it in its entirety and decide where the Start-Here point is.

Julie Castiglia, Literary Agent

If you want to write the setup for yourself, then go ahead and perhaps include it as a flashback if it is absolutely

necessary, but you might find that when you've finished
the book you can throw it in the trash.

Bob Silverstein, Literary Agent

Remember that guy in *The Plague* who dies perfecting the
first sentence of his novel: If the beginning keeps giving
you trouble, it may mean you should think about what
comes next.

Anonymous Senior Editor, Farrar, Straus and Giroux

"Call me Ishmael." That was a memorable opening. Too
many writers start off either with lengthy exposition
(boring!) or else endless inane dialogue without setting
up context. Don't be vague. Establish a clean sense of
time, place, and potential conflict. Write what you know.
Write from the heart.

Toni Weisskopf, Publisher, Baen Books

Robert A. Heinlein was a master of the great beginning.
Look at the first paragraph of his finest work, *The Moon Is
a Harsh Mistress*.

> I see in *Lunaya Pravda* that Luna City Council has passed
> on first reading a bill to examine, license, inspect—and
> tax—public food vendors operating inside municipal
> pressure. I see also is to be mass meeting tonight to or-
> ganize "Sons of Revolution" talk-talk.

Bang. So many goals achieved. The reader is made aware
the action is taking place in the future, when there is a

colony on the moon. The reader is made aware that the Cold War between the U.S. and the Soviet Union at the time the book was written has somehow changed and there is a multicultural society on the moon, just from the casual references to both a *Pravda* and a city council, and from the new argot used by the narrator. We are starting to get some idea of the narrator's character from his "and taxed" comment. And the reader is aware that this is to be a book about revolution. All in two sentences.

This does not start right in the middle of an action scene, and it doesn't need to. Heinlein is setting the stage for the revolution and the personal tragedy to happen to the narrator and there is no need to rush into that. His voice is unique and intriguing in itself.

Baen Books bought *Tinker* by Wen Spencer on the basis of three chapters and an outline. I was familiar with the author's reputation, but hadn't read any of her previously published fantasies. But when I encountered Tinker, the title character, I was intrigued. Here was a tough young woman keeping her head when thrust into the unknown, and attacking problems like a scientist, even though that problem was an elf-lord with hell-hounds on his trail invading her junkyard. Spencer took an old trope, elves, combined it with a parallel worlds concept, and threw in a great viewpoint character with a fascinating approach to life. Irresistible. And so the readers found; *Tinker* became a genre bestseller and we bought another book in the series.

Here's the first two paragraphs of the *Tinker* proposal partial:

> The wargs chased the elf over Pittsburgh Scrap and Salvage's tall chain-link fence shortly after the hyper-phase gate powered down.
>
> Tinker had been high up in the crane tower, shuffling cars around the dark sprawling maze of her scrap yard, trying to make room for the influx of wrecks Shutdown Day always brought in. Her cousin, Oilcan, was out with the flatbed wrecker, clearing their third call of the night and it wasn't Shutdown proper yet.

As with the Heinlein, the fantasy nature of the story comes out in the first line. The matter-of-fact way the viewpoint character takes the idea of Shutdown Day and elves and wargs is also a strong indication that this is a new take on urban fantasy. In the first two pages we see how Tinker deals with the problems in her scrap yard, so when the elves and wargs make it over the fence, we already have a feel for how she will react. And that's really all I needed to know this was going to be an interesting read.

Barbara Collins Rosenberg, Literary Agent

Avoid telling. Show the reader what is happening and avoid backstory. Placing comments through the text can accomplish the same thing as pages of history. I hate to harp on backstory, but pages and pages of it in the beginning are a turnoff to me. I sometimes advise writers to throw away their first three chapters and begin their books with chapter four.

Jodie Rhodes, President, Jodie Rhodes Literary Agency

We agents can seem downright callous at times. As one who used to be a writer, I know what you go through and how the rejections sting. But keep this in mind. Less than 20 percent of all the books published in a year are fiction, yet 90 percent of all the queries agents receive from writers are for novels.

Ever since the computer, it seems the whole world wants to write a novel. Your competition is your fellow writers.

So you have to learn how to interest us and you must learn humility. I can tell you that when an agent receives a query where the author announces how talented he or she is, how compelling their book, when they compare it to acclaimed best-selling authors, we know right away this is a loser.

Over and over again it has been shown that the more modest the writer, the better the writing. That's because good writers know how much they still have to learn.

If you do nothing more after reading this but polish the first page of your novel until it leaps off that page, filled with life, you will have advanced the chances of selling your book tenfold.

Good luck to you.

Jacky Sach, Co-founder, Bookends Literary Agency

With a changing world—fast-paced entertainment such as computer games, Internet chats, TV, movies, iPods, etc.—make sure you're competing on a very high level.

Mike Farris, Farris Literary Agency, Inc.

Remember that the beginning sets the tone for the reader. It tells the reader whether you can write, whether you can create a character, and whether you can tell a story. The most important sentence you will write is the first one. You make your first impression on the reader at the start, and you only get one chance to make that first impression. Don't waste it.

I can tell on the first page, the first paragraph, even, whether a writer can write. If the first page is poorly written and developed, I have no confidence that page 88 or page 267 or any other page will be any better.

These agents and editors and publishers are telling it straight. I'd pay attention!

EPILOGUE

Play the Game Forward

My son, Mike, is a talented baseball player, and I've helped coach him since he was a little guy. These days, he towers over me at about 6'2" (and is still growing at the age of sixteen) and is a better player than I ever dreamed of becoming when I was his age. I still give him one piece of coaching advice that I'd like to pass on to you as well, which I'll get to by and by, after my little ramble here. Bear with me if you will.

Mike's a pitcher, and sometimes bad things happen to pitchers no matter how well they're throwing. Sometimes, the guy on the mound will throw the perfect pitch and the batter will still drill it over the left-field wall for a dinger. Sometimes the pitcher induces a perfect ground ball to create a double play and get out of the inning and the shortstop fluffs it and both runners are safe. In times like those, Mike knows what I'm going to say to him.

"Play the game forward," I'll yell out to him. Yeah, yeah, he nods, turning his back on the mound to gather his thoughts and refocus. But I know that's exactly what he's thinking. To play the game forward. What's done is done, and we like to call that kind of thing ancient history. It does no one a bit of good to dwell on the past in the game of baseball, even if that past only happened seconds ago. Doesn't do much good in the game of writing, either.

The thing is, we've all made mistakes—writers and ballplayers alike—and it's more than likely that we'll all continue to make mistakes the rest of our lives. Another saying we use in the game of baseball is: "When you're green, you're growing; when you're ripe, you're rotten." Which clearly means that it's a good thing to be green and making mistakes, even dumb ones. It's the way we learn and the way we get better at whatever we're attempting, baseball or writing. Or, writing about baseball. Oops, sorry. My attempt at a joke! Gotta work on that humor thing.

Anyway, what I want to say here is that you may have read this book and at times thought, "Shoot! I did that red flag in the manuscript I sent out."

My comment on that is: So what?

That's ancient history. You don't get a redo in life after the age of say, ten or so. You made a boo-boo, perhaps, but it isn't the end of the world. Not for writers, so long as they keep manufacturing trees in the tree factory (or wherever they make them to produce that paper we use). It just means we needn't make the same mistake tomorrow. And, being a smart human bean, I know you won't.

Epilogue

Tomorrow, I'm pretty sure I'll discover I've been doing something in my writing craft that I shouldn't do. Or, I'll find a better way to do something. That doesn't mean what I did before I gained the new knowledge is worthless doo-doo. Not in the least.

I guess what I'm trying to say is don't stress over stuff. Do the best you can and keep moving forward. Your work will get better and better as long as you keep working at it.

Above all, don't fall victim to paralysis by overanalysis. Take what works for you from this book and forget what doesn't. Trust your instincts. (Except when they tell you to begin with backstory.) My wife, Mary, has a saying she coined in describing a friend of ours who was always avoiding opportunities in life by imagining the worst that could happen. "He creates ceilings to bump his head into." Don't you be like our friend!

As the famous Canadian part-time philosopher and full-time loafer Red Green says, "I'm pulling for ya. We're all in this together."

Play the game forward.

I'll be looking for you on the bookshelves.

INDEX

Index